WITHDRAWN

The Tie

Trends and Traditions

The Tie

Trends and Traditions

Sarah Gibbings

BARRON'S

First U.S. edition published 1990 by
Barron's Educational Series, Inc.

Text copyright © 1990 Sarah Gibbings/The Inside Page Limited
This edition © 1990 Studio Editions Ltd.

All inquiries should be addressed to
Barron's Educational Series, Inc.
250 Wireless Boulevard
Hauppauge, New York 11788

Designed and edited by
Anness Law Ltd,
4a The Old Forge
7 Caledonian Road
London N1 9DX

Series Editor: Madeleine Ginsburg

Ties on jacket front courtesy of
American Classics, Vintage Clothing,
20 Endell Street, London WC2
Tel: 071 831 1210

Photograph of Gary Cooper by Ross Verlag.

ISBN 0-8120-6199-3

Printed in Czechoslovakia

PICTURE ACKNOWLEDGMENTS

The author and publishers wish to acknowledge the following picture sources, and apologize for any omissions:

a=above, b=below, l=left, m=middle, r=right, t=top

[Names in parentheses indicate location of painting or work]
10a (Mauritshuis, The Hague), 12 (Pollock House, Glasgow), 13 (Norton Simon Museum), 14, 39l, 68 (National Portrait Gallery, London), 15 (Wallace Collection, London), 17b, 41, 45, 48, 53, 66 (Victoria and Albert Museum, London), 20r, 67 (Sotheby's London), 22 (Bibliothèque National, Estampes), 25tr (Musée du Louvre, Paris), 25tl, 28, 62, 88b (National Gallery, London), 26 (National Army Museum, London), 27b (Dallas Museum of Art), 30r (Cincinnati Museum of Art), 33 (Musée du Carnavalet, Paris), 35 (Tate Gallery, London), 36 (Private collection), 37 (Lauros Giraudon), 771 (Chicago Art Institute), 84bl (Detroit Institute of Art), 88a (Redfern Gallery, London), 90 (U.S.A. National Collection), 93, 142, 145b (Gieves and Hawkes), 108br (Royal Academy, London).

B.F.I. Stills, Posters and Designs: 100, 113a, 128r; Camera Press, London: 1381, 139; Hermès: 122b, 131t, 131r (Frederic Dumas), 131b, 140l (Sacha), 140r; Inside Page Collection, The: 69, 89a, 941 (Gallery of London), 95r (Gallery of London), 110, 115r, 116, 110, 120tl, 120b, 130, 132t, 132r, 134, 136, 143, 146, 147, 148r; J.S: 138r, 145t; Lord Lichfield, 96, 97; Madeleine Ginsburg: 78; Mary Evans Picture Library: 40b, 51, 71; Museum of London: 73b; Paul Smith: 141, 1481; Science Museum, London: 84a; Topham Picture Source: 64b, 87r, 102, 104a, 106, 107, 108a, 1151, 118, 123b, 124b, 125, 126, 127, 132bl; Vintage magazine: 38, 39r, 112, 114, 117, 121a, 129, 133.

Contents

Foreword

"After another lingering look he put the glass down and unlocked his leather jewel-case. In it were pins of all kinds, made with screw heads, so that they could serve indiscriminately as studs, and he turned them over. There was a beautiful ruby set in tiny brilliants, which he saw at once was the proper color for the tone of his dress. He had worn it as a solitaire the evening before, and he unscrewed it, and replaced the back of the stud with a pin. But then he stopped. Not long ago Kit had given him a charming turquoise of the *vieille roche*, a piece of noonday sky, and incapable of turning green. It would be suitable to wear that when he met her, but unfortunately it did not go at all well with his clothes. However, sentimental considerations prevailed, and he put the ruby back, pinned the turquoise into his tie, and looked at himself again. 'It is rather an experiment,' he said half aloud."

This charming picture of a young man in 1898 in a railway carriage en route for a weekend in the country, impressed me enormously with its chic when I read it as a nine-year-old. I found it again, without difficulty, in E.F. Benson's novel *Mammon and Co*, at the London Library. I still think it has style.

So has Miss Gibbing's monograph. It also has authenticity as her research has been carried out rigorously. She has, so to speak, tied up her Steinkerk (*Oxford Dictionary* spelling).

I forgive her, being a consumer, a giver of presents to friends and relatives, for focusing on shops like Gieves and Hawkes, and Lewins, in preference to manufacturers. Lewins is indeed a much revered specialist in club and regimental ties, and Gieves knows all there is to know about uniforms.

The most popular design for a tie at the moment (a moment which has already been ticking away for a year or two) is without question based on the Indian designs launched in the middle of the last century in Paisley, Scotland. Their coloring comes from that of the madder tree. The designs originate in Kashmir and are of course similar to those on Kashmir shawls. The silk used is known as gum-twill.

The doyen of makers of such silk is undoubtedly David Evans of England. They have existed since the 1840s, but it is since the beginning of the century that the Paisley or Foulard (the name given to a scarf of Indian design) has been worn by gentlemen extensively.

The prestigious Italian silk manufacturer, Ratti, is today selling quantities of English-looking Paisley silks. They sometimes are a little strange because they use classic Paisley designs put into totally "un-madder" coloring — chemical dyes instead of vegetable — another instance of clever marketing by Europeans of designs and styles originally English.

I opened my dress house in 1946. In 1950, we opened the boutique. In 1953 I ordered some men's ties to sell in it. I ordered "Four-in-Hands" made of a square of silk, folded into the shape of the tie, the silk of the tie forming the lining as well as the tie itself. This is the most luxurious form of neckwear existing in my lifetime. These beautiful ties lay unloved and unwanted among the ladies' gloves, blouses, and necklaces until one day Hans Wallach, the head of the necktie manufacturing firm called Michelsons (from whom I had ordered the "Four-in-Hands") asked me to work with him in making a collection of ties to be sold throughout England and the world. In 1961, I signed a contract which is still flourishing today. I think we were just before Cardin, certainly neck and neck, or necktie and necktie.

It was of course the beginning of the menswear licensee business for us: now known as the "designer label" operation. Ours is completely genuine in the sense that my staff and I are involved in the design of ties that bear our label. At this very moment, a fellow director is with the present head of Michelsons in Como, buying tie silk for 1991. We have already decided that ties should be of a width of 9½ cms at the base. This is ½ cm wider than those currently on sale. The width of the shoulders of the suit have influenced this decision. We have decided on muted, as distinct from loud colors; the British look demands this. Paisley designs are still there, and so are regimental and club stripes, but masculine and virile colors creep into the stripes when the background is sombre.

From a success with Michelsons in London — and success is measured by the degree to which a designer's name becomes so firmly established that it is unattractively called a "brand" name, we have spread to the United States, Canada, Australia, New Zealand, Japan, Korea, and Taiwan. Germany and France refuse to admit that there are English dress designers. The French indeed often show surprise that we do not still wear woad.

I cannot here expand on the importance of the tie in a man's toilet. It certainly reveals his taste and, I believe, his character. The suit is still very much the uniform of the man who is brought up to conform with the traditions of civilized European life. The details of the suit, the shape of the collar, the placing and numbering of buttons all have a history. Any marked deviation is noticed and usually rejected. The story of it all is too long for this essay.

The choice of the silk of the tie, its color and its size, be it of the blade or the knot, are very personal matters. The light-reflecting silk lightens the effect of the usually sombre colors of the wool cloth of the suit. It is of vast importance to the total costume. It comes into a room almost before the man.

SIR HARDY AMIES

Shih Huang Ti's Legacy: 221 B.C.–the 17th Century

Above: A terracotta soldier, one of Shih Huang Ti's Terracotta army wearing one of the first known neckties, a carefully wrapped cloth of silk. 221 BC.

It was a humid September morning in 1974 when a group of Chinese peasants set out for a hillock in the fields near the ancient capital city of Xi'an to dig a new well. As they sweated over their pickaxes and shovels, they only had one thought in their minds — finding a new source of clean water for their village, which they could drink safely, use to irrigate their crops and generally ease the grinding poverty of their daily lives during Chairman Mao Tse Tung's Cultural Revolution. They neither wanted nor expected to find anything else under Mount Li, and when one pick struck clean through a layer of stone and opened the way into a hidden cavern, they merely hoped that they had discovered an underground river.

In fact, they had stumbled on the tomb of China's first emperor, Shih Huang Ti, containing the world-famous "terracotta army" – and evidence of the first known necktie. Under the rubble and mud in the vault they had opened lay some 7,500 of the emperor's sculptured soldiers, each wearing a carefully wrapped neckcloth.

Shih Huang Ti — alternatively known as Qin Shi Huangdi — was a warlord who had succeeded in unifying China and founding the Qin dynasty in 221 B.C. He was a fierce and ambitious man who relished battle and thought nothing of forcibly recruiting millions of his countrymen to build the Great Wall and the network of roads which allowed his troops to move quickly around his empire. But he was afraid of one thing — death. He did his best to find some way of avoiding it, sending messengers to Tibet and India in search of a miraculous elixir that would allow him to stay on his throne forever.

Finally, when he realized that he would inevitably die like other men, he began to build a magnificent tomb near his capital city. At first, he intended to slaughter an entire army, who would then accompany him through eternity, but he was eventually persuaded to make do with their life-sized replicas modeled in terracotta. The greatest sculptors and artists from every province in China were summoned to create this massive monument to one man's fear and folly, and were set to work forming legions of archers, horsemen, footsoldiers and officers. Each figure was unique, and every detail of armor, hair and costume was reproduced meticulously. And when Shih Huang Ti died in 210 B.C., during a routine round of inspection, he was placed in this extraordinary mausoleum and forgotten.

What is remarkable about the discovery of the 7,500 soldiers wearing their 7,500 neckcloths is that they are an archeological and iconographic freak. No other pictures or statues of Chinese — or, indeed, of any other people — would show any evidence of neckcloths for centuries to come.

Chinese looms of that period were certainly able to weave silk of the right width for the neckcloths worn by the terracotta army; and records show that in 16 B.C., during the reign of Ch'eng Ti, the frontier garrison was given one million rolls of silk 32 feet 9 inches (10 m) long and 1 foot 8 inches (53 cm) wide. But only Shih Huang Ti's personal guard seem to have wrapped material around their necks. Why should they have done something so bizarre?

This mystery is mirrored by the equally strange case of the Roman soldiers sculpted on the marble Column of Trajan in Rome. This was erected near the Piazza Venezia in A.D. 113 by Marcus Ulpius Trajanus — better known as Trajan — to commemorate his victories against the Dacians, who lived in what is now Romania. It features some 2,500 realistic figures of legionnaires engaged in the most important battles of the campaign. Some of these soldiers are sculpted in low relief, and the largest of them, which are about 24–28 inches (60–70 cm) high, are wearing neckcloths. Some have wound a piece of material around their necks and tucked it into their armor; others have knotted kerchiefs, cowboy-style; while still another group sport short, primitive versions of the modern four-in-

Above: A section of Trajan's Column in Rome, AD113. The legionaries, who are sculpted in low relief, wear neckcloths, probably to protect themselves from the sun during their long and arduous campaigns. The neckcloths are tied in various ways: some are wound around the neck and tucked into the armor, others are knotted, cowboy-style; yet others are short, primitive versions of the modern four-in-hand tie.

Above: *Portrait of a Married Couple* by P. Codde (1599–1678) in which the man is wearing an exquisite lace collar and the woman a broad fine ruff.

Below: A self-portrait by G. ter Borch (1617–81) in which the artist sports a collar inside a delicate lacy cravat.

Opposite page: This plate from Racinet's *Le Costume Historique* shows Malays, Papuans and Australian Aborigines sporting a wide range of neckwear made variously of beads, shells and bone.

hand tie in a soft, lightweight material.

For centuries, these figures were generally thought to prove that the Romans had begun the practice of twisting, knotting or tying material around the neck, and some authorities — notably H. Le Blanc, author of the definitive guide to early 19th-century neckware, *The Art of Tying the Cravat* — even attributed a range of neckwear to Roman civilians as well.

The Romans kept their throats warm "by means of a woollen or silken cloth, called in Rome *focalium*, a term which is evidently derived from *fauces* (the throat)," wrote Le Blanc in 1828. He also cites the Jesuit scholar Father Guillaume Adam, who apparently claimed that Roman orators who were worried about losing their voices made neckcloths fashionable. Some, says Le Blanc, used a handkerchief, or *sudarium*, which he believes to be the prototype for the cravat and the reason why "in many countries" modern neckcloths were referred to as "neckhandkerchiefs." However, he then goes on to insist that, at various stages in Roman history, it was considered beneath the dignity "of the man and citizen" to cover his throat "except by hand, or occasionally wrapping the toga around it." The Roman writers Horace, Seneca and Quintilian provide further evidence for this, claiming that neckcloths were the mark of sickly or effeminate men.

Despite this range of references, the Column of Trajan is the only *visual* reminder of the Roman fashion. Clearly, wearing a neckcloth was neither normal nor even socially desirable among Roman citizens — so why did the proud legionnaires of the Dacian campaign sport an item of clothing that marked them out as unusual in a potentially negative way?

The answer to the mysteries of the neckwear of both the Chinese and Roman soldiers is simple. Their neckcloths were telling observers: "I am special."

For the Chinese, they were a mark of the singular honor bestowed on them by the emperor, who had chosen them as models for the effigies that would accompany him through eternity. For the Romans, they were a way of putting over a more complex message: "Neckcloths may normally be worn by wimps, but I am such an acclaimed soldier that I do not need to be bothered with the usual rules. For me, this adornment is a mark of my unusual success."

Underlining this hierarchical message would have been the understanding that cloth was too precious a resource to be wasted on something as unnecessary as a neckcloth. Most people simply could not afford to use material, which could have made a perfectly good jacket or toga, on a neck adornment. The widespread adoption of neckwear had to wait until cloth was plentiful and cheap enough.

In using neckwear as a mark of status, the Chinese and Romans were merely following a tradition as old as mankind. In hot climates such as those of the South American jungles, African plains or Pacific islands, clothing had always been restricted to a small loin cloth or apron, while feathers, beads, stones and shells had been strung around the neck to indicate a person's wealth and importance. Neckwear also had a symbolic function, in that it was used to signal tribal and social adherence in addition to status, occupation and wealth. A necklace of different shells, or shells of different sizes or in different combinations, could indicate which tribe a man came from, whether he was married, whether he had heirs as well as showing that he was a chieftain, a landowner or a warrior. The richer the society or culture, the richer the neckwear became. For instance, the ancient Egyptian pharaohs who ruled some 4,000 years ago wore broad neckbands of precious metal and stones to complement their simple linen robes.

The main upholders of this primitive tradition, until the comparative wealth of 16th- and 17th-century Europe made neckwear commonplace, were priests and other religious functionaries.

Tibetan Buddhist monks have for centuries worn *katas*, scarflike strips of silk

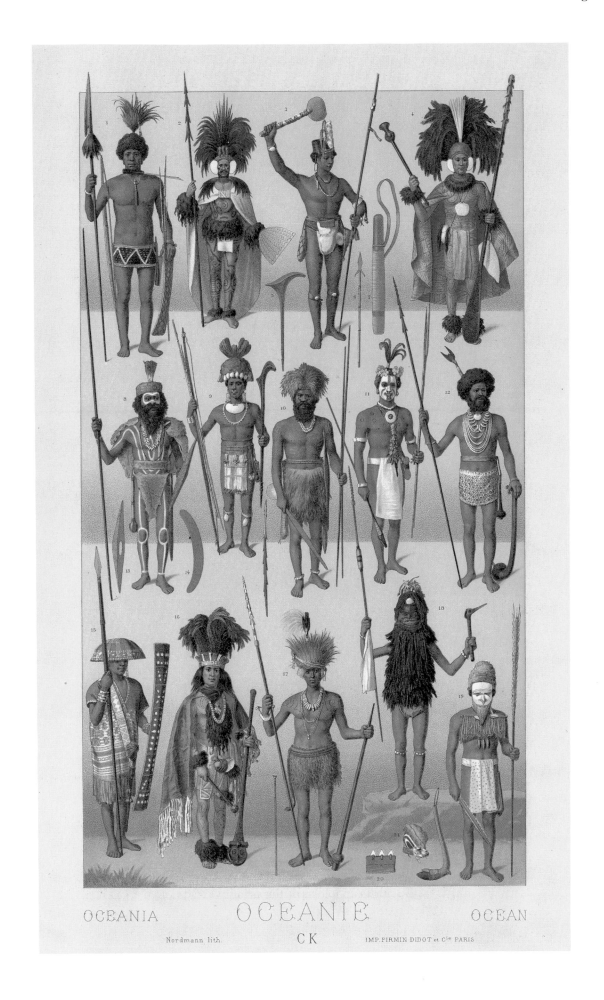

OCEANIA OCEANIE OCEAN

Nordmann lith. CK IMP. FIRMIN DIDOT et Cᵢₑ PARIS

Right: *Portrait of a Man* by El Greco (1541–1614). The austerity of this doublet is alleviated by the gentleman's enormous ruff or millstone collar of pleated linen. Throughout the 16th century, as the frill that had adorned the collar of a shirt became larger and larger, ruffs reached enormous proportions.

or cotton gauze 3–6 feet (0.9–1.8 m) long. These are given to the priests by visitors to their temples and at weddings, and to the host in a private house. Some present-day monks believe that they were derived from the neckcloths worn by the high-caste troops who modeled for Shih Huang Ti's terracotta army.

The Jewish prayer shawl, or *tallith*, is a fringed garment with a purely symbolic function, worn by a man over his shoulders while he is praying. Like the *kata*, the *tallith* has been, for much of its history, an extravagance only justifiable in terms of spiritual necessity.

The other ceremonial religious garment that was designed to formalize neckwear and endow it with special hierarchical importance is the Christian priest's stole. In Roman times, a Christian preacher dressed himself in lay clothing and only stressed his special position as a minister of God by putting a *pallium* (a sort of cloak used by orators) over his shoulders while addressing his congregation. This cloak gradually dwindled and metamorphosed, first into a mantle, then a folded wrap, before finally, toward the end of the 4th century A.D., becoming the narrow, rigid scarf — or stole — we recognize today.

For centuries, religion was the only area in which neckscarfs or cloths had any role to play. Some scholars have suggested that the colors or favors worn on the helms or at the necks of medieval knights to signify their allegiance foreshadowed modern club and regimental ties, but in general, the wealthy draped gold chains and jewels around their necks while the poor were too involved in the struggle to keep alive to worry about neckwear.

The Renaissance was crucial to the development of formal neckwear not because it reintroduced neckcloths, but because it confirmed men in their taste for rich and extravagant clothing in brilliant colors. From the 14th century onward, and despite the advent of Martin Luther and the puritanical Protestant churches, men indulged in every sartorial whim: silk stockings in different colors; velvet, brocade and jeweled doublets; feathered hats; and gold and silver trims. However, the condemnation — by Martin Luther and others — of wealth, luxury and corruption made such extravagance seem excessive, and as time passed, the bright colors and voluptuous materials began to fade away.

It seemed as if men's days as peacocks were coming to an end — which was when the attractions of neckwear became apparent. If a man could not demonstrate his wealth, taste and individuality on the larger canvas of the clothes on his

Left: ***Portrait of a Painter* by Frans Hals (*c*1580–1666). The artist wears a simple linen collar of the type often worn by Puritans. Norton Simon Museum.**

Above: James II by an unknown portraitist. The monarch is shown wearing a Venetian lace cravat.

back, he could at least wear fine linen and expensive lace at his throat.

The beginnings of the modern necktie can be discerned in the tying strings used during the reign of King Henry VII in England to bring together the necks of the rather *décolleté* shirts then in favor. These strings could be seen above the top of the doublet. In the time of Henry VIII, the collar of the shirt formed a little frill; and as the 16th century wore on, the frill became larger and larger until Queen Elizabeth I's courtiers wore ruffs of pleated linen or lace the size of dinner plates.

By the time the doomed King Charles I was on the throne, neckwear itself became a focus for political and moral controversy. Oliver Cromwell and his puritan Model Army — like the Pilgrim Fathers who took their simple linen collars and sternly egalitarian philosophy to the New World of America in 1620 — flaunted their plain and unadorned neckwear as a direct reproach to the unbridled extravagance, both material and spiritual, of the Royalists. Their enormous ruffs, succeeded by hanging collars, falling bands of linen and lace, which at one point were large and lavish enough to cover their shoulders, vanished with their temporary defeat in the English Civil War of 1642–1649.

The reasons for the appearance of cravats around the time of the Thirty Years' War (1618–1648) in Europe and at the restoration of Charles II to the English throne in 1660 are more complex and confused.

Some authorities, such as Penelope Byrde of the Bath Museum of Costume in southwest England, believe that the cravat evolved naturally from falling bands. During the 1630s, Byrde suggests, it became fashionable for aristocratic men to wear their hair longer, to make a statement about their political and religious loyalties which were directly opposed to those of the crop-haired Puritans, commonly known as Roundheads. Later, as the court of Louis XIV, the Sun King (who reigned from 1643 to 1715), became the focus of Europe, lace became the most desirable and costly of materials, especially the prized lace of Flanders and Venice. When men grew their hair to shoulder length, or adopted long wigs, the beautiful lace of their collars was covered, and so they simply knotted the collar-ends together to display the lace to its best advantage.

Those adhering to this theory often claim that the word *cravat* is a corruption of *rabat* — another name for a hanging collar or falling bands. Others point out that references to cravats occur well before this time. The French poet Eustache Deschamps, who lived in the late 14th and early 15th centuries, wrote in a ballad, *"faites restraindre sa cravate"* ("tighten his cravat"), as A. Varron noted in an article published in March 1941 in *Ciba Review*. And the engraver Cesare Vecellio used the word *cravatta* to describe the ancient Roman *focalium* in his book *Degli abiti antichi e moderni in diverse parti del mondo* (*Ancient and Modern Dress in Various Parts of the World*) in 1590.

However, the traditional explanation for the emergence of the cravat is more romantic. When, in 1618, Sweden and France began their battle across Europe against the Hapsburg Empire, which was to become known as the Thirty Years' War, Croatian mercenaries (who often also included Bosnians and Hungarians) were brought in by Louis XIII. (His successors were to continue to engage a regiment known as the *Cravate Royale* until the French Revolution of 1789). By the 1650s, European noblemen were being painted wearing knotted scarfs, jabots and bow-tied neckwear, generically termed cravats, and there were shops in Paris stocking lace scarves, jabots and kerchiefs to knot around the neck. Later authors jumped to the obvious conclusion — that "cravat" is a corruption of "Croat" and this must have been the form of neckwear favored by the mercenary troops.

H. Le Blanc, for example, was so smitten with the legend of the East European soldiers that he muddled the date of the cravat's arrival in England — it was actually brought by the returning Charles II and his courtiers in 1660, after they had spent nine years in exile in the French court — with the arrival in France of the Croats themselves. "In 1660 a regiment of Croats arrived in France," he declares in *The Art of Tying the Cravat*.

A part of their singular costume excited the greatest admiration, and was immediately and generally imitated; this was a *tour de cou*, made (for private soldiers) of common lace, and of muslin or silk for the officers; the ends were arranged *en rosette*, or ornamented with a button or tuft, which hung gracefully on the breast.

Officers and people of rank, he continues, wore cravats with embroidered ends or trimmed "with broad lace." The lower classes had cloth or cotton cravats, "or at the best of black taffeta, pleated: which was tied round the neck with two small strings."

Below: The family of Louis XIV by Largillierre (1656–1746). The men wear expensive long cravats which would have cost more than the average annual wage of the day.

In fact, there are several other, equally plausible linguistic and etymological sources for the word. The Turkish *kyrabacs* and the Hungarian *korbacs* both mean "whip" or "long, slender object," as does the French *cravache*. Any of these words could have been used to describe the slender twists of material that became known as cravats.

Whatever its true history, the cravat was well and truly established by the

LACE

Belgian folklore boasts a wonderfully romantic story to explain the invention of lace. A medieval knight, runs the legend, went off to fight in the Crusades against the infidel in the East and left his lady a rose as a token of his love. As the rose wilted and the petals fell apart, the lady embroidered them together again with fine white thread. Eventually the flower crumbled to dust; she was left with lace to remind her of her lover.

Sadly, this story is nonsense. Lace is known to have been made in Egyptian times, some fine examples having been found in pyramid tombs. By the 16th century, ornate, needlemade lace had evolved. This was formed as a series of buttonhole stitches packed together in solid patterns against a background of open buttonholes or loop stitches.

Venetian lace – also known as *gros point* or *point de Venise* – was the most desirable of this kind of lace, and became the ultimate material for the early cravats of the 17th century. The cloth had an almost three-dimensional effect, created by its bold patterns of closed buttonholes joined by picot stitches, or small loops. Venetian *rose point*, invented during the 17th century, was a smaller version of *gros point*, with star, rose and snowflake patterns made out of buttonhole stitches.

Above: This late 17th-century portrait of William of Orange by an unknown artist shows him wearing a *point de Venise* cravat.

Other fashionable cravat laces were *point de France* – which was softer than Venetian lace and had slightly raised points with hexagonal bars joined by picots — and Cluny lace, which actually came from Genoa, and included floral motifs and plaited bars forming the *toile*, or solid part of the design.

Later in the 17th century, lighter bobbin laces were invented. These looked like woven muslin nets crossed with twisted threads forming delicate patterns. The most favored of the bobbin laces were Belgian Binche, Mechlin, Valenciennes and *point d'Angeleterre*, and designs incorporated roses, lillies, carnations, fruit blossoms, tulips, suns and moons, coats of arms, hunting scenes and cherubs.

Europe went mad for lace in the 17th and 18th centuries. Needle- and bobbinmade laces were used to trim bed linen, underskirts and overskirts, and to make collars, cuffs and cravats. The more lace you possessed, and the more places you could find to display it, the more fashionable you were.

As the 17th century progressed, the appetite for lace got out of control. Laces became more covetable if they came from other countries, but because of the high customs duties and trade restrictions imposed, there was much smuggling of the most desirable Belgian and Venetian laces into countries such as France, Spain and England. A Royal Proclamation forbade "the selling in England, or the importation after June 24th 1662, of any foreign bone-lace, cutwork, fringe, buttons or needlework made of thread, silk or either of them."

The diarist Samuel Pepys was one of many who broke the law, buying imported lace for a cravat at Cheapside in London on 12 October 1663. He wrote in his diary that it cost "more than [sic] 20 s[hillings] than I intended; but when I came to see them I was resolved to buy one worth wearing with credit." Pepys, the son of a poor tailor, had enjoyed a university education, and was very keen to keep up with gentlemanly fashion. Finally, friends told him (in 1669) that he had gone too far — a civil servant with the Admiralty Board, they informed him, should not wear gold lace.

Each country responded to the lace fever by encouraging its own lace-making industry. Count Lorenzo Magalotti, visiting Devonshire in southwest England in 1669, noted, "There is not a cottage in all the county nor in that of Somerset [a neighboring county] where white lace is not made in great quantities; so that not only the whole kingdom is supplied with it, but it is exported in great abundance."

Above: Detail of exquisite *point de France*, **late 17th century.**

Below: Fine Belgian lace cut from a cravat. 17th century.

This trend did not diminish the attraction of foreign lace. In 1678, the Marquis de Nesmond seized a boat laden with 744,953 ells (1 ell = 45 inches/1.1 m) of Flemish lace bound for England. At about the same time, the Belgians had begun to call their lace *point d'Angleterre*, in the hope that it would be mistaken for the home-made product by the English authorities. The ruse did not work.

Smuggling between Flanders and France was easier. It was known for a dog to be wrapped like a mummy in lace, then dressed in a false coat, taken to the border and released, to be collected on the other side. The major danger with this scheme was losing the dog.

The passion for lace cravats waned during the course of the 18th century, although lace-ruffled shirt fronts and wrist frills remained fashionable until late in the century. When, in 1804, Napoleon wore a lace cravat, or jabot, for his imperial coronation, it was considered anachronistic — by this time, the fine cravats of a previous age were being reused as trimming for women's clothes.

Now only ceremonial reminders of the great age of lace neckwear remain. Scotsmen in their dress kilts would feel undressed without a lace jabot, while Black Rod still wears a lace cravat at the State Opening of the British Parliament.

Right: A limewood carving of a cravat by Grinling Gibbons, extraordinary in its detail – and typical of his finest work. Late 17th century.

mid-17th century, and in the French court it had accrued its own set of rituals. In the reign of Louis XIV, those members of the king's household responsible for His Majesty's *toilette* were much envied, and the *cravatier*, or the man responsible for the care of the royal cravats, was one of the most important of these trusted individuals. His job was to present a selection of cravats to the wardrobe master, who would help to choose the relevant piece of cloth. He would then straighten the king's collar and help with the draping and tying of the cravat. Although the king reserved for himself the privilege of tying the final knot, the *cravatier* was expected to add the finishing touches, including craven praise of the result. He might also fold the cloth to the requisite width and deal with brooches and other adornments for the cravat.

"*Après que le cravatier a présenté la cravate au grand-maître de la garde-robe, il accomode le col de la chemise du Roy,*" says the *Dictionnaire historique des arts, métiers et professions*, published in France in 1906.

La cravate mise, s'il apperçoit quelqu'endroit qui n'aille pas assez bien, il y met encore la main. En l'absence de ses supérieurs, il met la cravate au Roy. Il attache tous les matins les diamans et les manchettes au poignets des chemise de Sa Majesté; il a entre ses mains toutes les cravates, les manchettes et tous les points et les dentelles pour le linge du Roy. Il plie les cravates de Sa Majesté et y noue les rubans, afin qu'elles soient toujours prêtes à mettre.

It was this reverence for the cravat and its rituals that the court brought back to England when Charles II reclaimed his throne in 1660. Once again it was fashionable to show off your wealth and style by larding your neck with extravagant lace. Charles himself is said to have horrified the more parsimonious of his subjects by spending 20 pounds and 12 shillings on a lace cravat — this at a time when a few pounds a year would have been considered a good salary.

There is a splendid story about the great wood carver Grinling Gibbons (1648–1721) who apparently thought the obsession with this new French fashion was so absurd that, in 1669, he parodied it by carving an immaculate wooden copy of a Venetian lace cravat for his friend Horace Walpole to wear at a reception given in honor of illustrious French visitors. The foreigners and their retinue were amazed at this, although too polite to comment openly, and went away convinced that the peculiar English made a habit of wearing wooden neckwear. Sadly, this must be a later legend as Walpole would only have been a boy at the time, but the carved cravat does exist and can be seen at the Victoria and Albert Museum in London.

The playwright Sir George Etherege was more directly scathing of the fashion. "That a man's excellency should lie in Neatly tying of a Ribbon, or a Cravat!" he sneered in Act I, Scene 1 of his 1676 play *The Man of Mode*. However, Charles' successor, James II, was undeterred. For his coronation in 1685, he ordered a Venetian lace cravat which cost a staggering 36 pounds and 10 shillings.

This obsession with Venetian lace — otherwise known as *gros point* or *point de Venise* — led to a fashion among those who wished to be thought wealthy enough to afford it. The material was so heavy that it could not be knotted in a bow or twisted as an ordinary cravat of linen and lighter lace could be, and it was therefore held in place with a ribbon. Those who wished to ape their superiors — or those rich enough to squander a small fortune on a cravat — took to tying their

Above and below left: Two men wearing precisely the kind of heavy Venetian lace cravat parodied so neatly by Grinling Gibbons in his limewood carving opposite.

cravats with ribbons too, thus paying careful tribute to the new style of the king and his friends.

Eventually this became a trend in its own right. H. Le Blanc speaks of "bright coloured ribands arranged in bows" when he discusses the development of neckwear in the 17th century. By the late 1680s, men were tying their cravat strings or ribbons in a wide bow under the cravat. This bow was designed to be seen, peeping out beneath the edges of the lacy neckcloth, and clearly foreshadows the solitaire, which was to become so popular in the mid-18th century.

Fads and fashions in neckwear multiplied so fast that by 1688 Randle Holme was complaining, in *The Academye of Armourie*, that the "cravatt" was meant to be simply an:

> . . . adornment for the neck being nothing else but a long Towel put about the Collar, and so tyed before with a Bow knot, this is the Original of all Such

Right: Portrait of a young gentleman holding a sporting gun with a dog by his side. Attributed to Francis Barlow. The cravat worn by the young man is a lace-edged cravat.

Wearing; but now by the Art of Invention of the Seamsters, there is so many new ways of making them, that it would be a Task to name them, much more to describe them.

The Steinkirk and colonial developments

Above the cravat strings, the neckcloth itself was becoming longer as the century progressed. For instance, the effigy of Charles II in Westminster Abbey, London, shows a cravat 34 inches (86 cm) long and 6 inches (15 cm) wide. The cravat itself could be self-tied, twisted, knotted, or folded. Lighter types of lace, such as Mechlin, were coming into frequent use, while muslin or lawn cravats with fringed or knotted ends were beginning to appear, foreshadowing the Steinkirk, a style which was to become a classic, lasting well into the 18th century.

The Steinkirk (also known as the Steenkirk) was a long, scarflike cravat with lace or fringing at the ends. It was worn loosely wrapped around the neck, with one end either tucked through a coat buttonhole (usually on the left breast) or pinned to the coat or waistcoat with a brooch. It took its name from the battle of Steinkirke in Holland in 1692, part of the War of the League of Augsburg. Legend has it that, when the British launched a surprise attack on Louis XIV's troops, the French soldiers had no time to arrange their cravats properly before fighting and therefore whisked the dangling ends, which might have gotten in their way, into their buttonholes. However, it is worth remembering that new fashions were, in that era, often simply named after recent events.

The passion for cravats spread steadily from Europe to the colonies, and by the end of the century, no gentleman from Plymouth, Devon or Plymouth, Massachusetts, would have dared to be seen in public, much less have his portrait painted, without the correct, preferably lace, neckwear. At this early stage in America's history, however, life for the settlers was comparatively harsh, and fashion did not originate in the New World but, inevitably, came from Europe. Indeed, American contributions to neckwear fashion were, until well into the 20th century, almost entirely limited to a relaxing of formal European styles, to make them more practical in the more extreme climates found there, where even gentlemen — or aspiring gentlemen — had to endure physical labor if they were to survive and thrive. Communications, too, were poor, with ships often taking months to reach the settlements. And when tools, seeds, building materials and

Above: A portrait of a gentleman by an unknown engraver. The man is wearing a loosely tied Steinkirk that complements the flowing style of the rest of his costume.

COLONIAL NECKWEAR

Neckwear was cherished by settlers in the fledgling colonies of America because of the scarcity of the materials for such luxuries. Even the Puritans – who were not supposed to be unduly concerned about appearances – could be extraordinarily passionate about their plain linen collars.

One poor girl, Mary Downing, made the mistake of singeing her brother's bands — the rectangular hanging collars which were the precursors of the cravat — and was rebuked so sternly by her stepmother that she wrote her father a pathetic letter:

Father, I trust that I have not provoked you to harbour soe ill an opinion of mee as my mothers . . . that I should abuse your goodness, and bee prodigall of yor purse, neglectful of my brothers bands . . . For my brothers bands I will not excuse myselfe, but I think not worthy such a sharpe reproofe . . .

And a Maryland gentleman bequeathed in his will of 1642: "Nine lace strips, nine quoifes, one coll, eight crosse-cloths . . . " Neckcloths of any type were often called cross-cloths or cross-cloathes at this time.

Above: The Royal Family Apartment at Versailles by Trouvain, *c*1694–98. The Steinkirk, sported by all the men except one, was then at the height of popularity.

even more human beings were the crucial imports, it was a mark of some self-indulgence and extravagance to order fashionable materials and apparel from the Old Country.

There are very few surviving portraits of colonial working men in their daytime neckwear although records of sailors wearing scarves and kerchiefs, which showed under their soft, turned-down collars, do exist. Still, some men were determined not to become bumpkins, and the first cravats with bows were imported into America as early as 1665, apparently in the luggage of new settlers arriving in the Boston area. Knotted cravats were especially popular, perhaps because they were easier to arrange when gentlemen were bereft of servants, elegant mirrors and well-run laundries.

The ultimate success of the Steinkirk in America was foreshadowed by the popularity of English dramatist and architect Sir John Vanbrugh's play *The Relapse*, first seen by Americans in 1697. It contained many useful pointers on fashionable garb back in England, among them an exchange between a seamstress and her customer.

SEAMSTRESS. I hope your lordship is pleased with your Steinkirk.
HIS LORDSHIP [*with eloquence*]. In love with it, stab my vitals! Bring your bill, you shall be paid tomorrow!

Alice Morse Earle, in *Two Centuries of Costume in America* (1910), traces examples of the kinds of brooches designed to fix the ends of the Steinkirk: "sometimes topaz, moonstone, garnet, marcasite, heliotropium, or paste." The Steinkirk

Left: This picture of the Comte de Toulouse by an unknown engraver, *c*1680s, shows a slightly lighter style of lace cravat.

persisted among old-fashioned American men until the 1770s and could still, according to Doriece Colle in her book *Collars, Stocks, Cravats* be found as late 1800, although the name itself went out of fashion by the end of the 17th century.

THE FIRST AMERICAN CRAVATS

The first cravats to be worn in America were considerably plainer than the fabulous lace creations favored in Europe, but they were still luxurious by the standards of the colonists.

The historian Alice Morse Earle describes a typical American interpretation of the new neckcloth, as worn by "the handsomest man in the Plantations," William Coddington, Governor of Providence and Rhode Island Plantation:

It consisted of a long scarf of soft, fine, sheer, white linen over two yards long, passed twice or thrice close around the throat and simply lapped under the chin, not knotted. The upper end hung from twelve to sixteen inches long. The other and larger end was carried down to a low waistline and tucked in between the buttons of the waistcoat.

Occasionally more lavish cravats were seen, but the plainer styles predominated. "Often the free end of this scarf was trimmed with lace or cutwork," Earle adds. "Indeed, the whole scarf might be of embroidery or lace, but the simpler lawn or mull appears to have been in better taste."

Revolutions: the 18th Century

Above: *The Countess of Mar* by **Kneller. The Countess is shown wearing a loosely tied Steinkirk.**

The original 17th-century cravat was a neckcloth for the élite — an expensive confection of fine white lace, linen or muslin which demanded a host of servants to launder and press and an infinite amount of time to arrange. As a means of demonstrating wealth and a leisured lifestyle, this style persisted until early in the 18th century, when British drapers' records show, for example, lace for cravats at 21 shillings a yard in 1700, the same price that was charged for a lady's scarlet Steinkirk in 1703. The simpler, less extravagant forms of cravat survived as fashionable neckwear well into the 1740s in Europe. They were also popular among the more practical, less comfortably off American colonists throughout the 18th century.

While the Steinkirk and other similarly loosely draped strips of linen muslin continued to be worn by conventional middle- and upper-class European men throughout the first half of the century, a new development in neckwear was proving irresistible to young sporting bucks who wished to show their independent attitude, toughness and fitness. The stock, originally developed for foot soldiers in France and Germany, rapidly became the only possible neckwear for the man of action — civilian as well as soldier — before sweeping to mass popularity, which would last well into the 1780s.

It was a simple high collar — at first made of black horsehair and, later, of whale-bone, pig-bristle, card, pasteboard or wood covered in cloth — which forced men to hold their heads high and thrust their chins out, giving them a martial and formal appearance. Another side effect was to make the poor soldiers who wore them rather red in the face — something which, legend has it, the king of Prussia felt was a thoroughly good thing, since this gave his troops the appearance of ruddy good health.

All in all, the stock was extremely uncomfortable and unhealthy, even later when, as it was taken up by the mass of men, it was padded and covered in military-style black silk or civilian white cotton or linen. H. Le Blanc was vehement in his disapproval. It was the Duc de Choiseul, minister of war under Louis XV, he believed, who first presented black horsehair stocks to French troops early in the 18th century. These items were, he writes, "tolerably hard, moderately wide, and were only injurious when fastened too tightly." Unfortunately, the military authorities were not content to leave the stock as a hard-wearing piece of uniform that would encourage the wearer to adopt a better

Above: A portrait of a gentleman by Antoine Watteau *c*1720. The fine lacy stock perfectly complements the beautiful brocade work on the waistcoat and jacket and the fine shirt cuffs.

Above left: *La Barn and Other Musicians* by A.H.R. Toumieres. 1707. The musicians are wearing elaborate soft cravats with knotted and fringed ends.

Below: A portrait of Sir George Cooke by Joseph Wright of Derby, *c*1767, in which the sitter wears a black lacy cravat knotted around his neck.

posture. "In many regiments," Le Blanc fumes,

> the officers wishing the men to appear healthy, obliged them to tighten the stock so as almost to produce suffocation, instead of allowing them more nourishing food, or of treating them with more kindness; or, in short, of giving them an opportunity of acquiring that health, the appearance only of which was produced by the tightened stock.

Life did not improve for soldiers around the world as the style caught on. "Each change has rendered it more injurious," Le Blanc observes.

> It has been transformed into a collar as hard as iron, by the insertion of a slip of wood, which acting on the larynx, and compressing every part of the neck, caused the eyes almost to start from their spheres, and gave the wearer a supernatural appearance often producing vertigo and faintings, or at least bleeding at the nose.
>
> It rarely happened that a field-day passed over without surgical aid being required by one or more soldiers, whose illness was only produced by an over-tightened stock.

To make matters worse, economies in military budgets resulted in stocks being issued in only one size, which made it impossible for many soldiers to move — and fight — naturally. The common soldier, Le Blanc concludes angrily, "was scarcely able to obey the order 'right face — left face,' and was entirely prohibited from stooping."

But the stock did have a number of distinct advantages over the more comfortable cravat. It was extremely easy to put on, since it was readymade and

Above: *The Death of Colonel Moorhouse* by R. Home, 1791. The black military stock was uniform wear for soldiers throughout the 18th and early 19th centuries, and led to the fashion for white linen civilian stocks, and ultimately to King George IV's black silk and velvet evening stock, the Royal George.

fastened at the back either with strings or with a buckle, and it was economical. A good stock collar could be re-covered a number of times in whatever material was preferred — originally always black satin, and later, linen, cotton, muslin, silk or calico. It also showed dirt less than the cravat.

The stock was adaptable as well. If the wearer wanted to display his individual taste, he either tied a length of material in a bow at the front of his neck or sewed one on. Other variations mimicked earlier draped cravat styles. If a man wanted to show that, despite his workmanlike neckwear, he was a person of wealth, he would wear a lavish stock buckle, which was usually, although not invariably, hidden under his wig at the back of his neck. Stock buckles in gold, silver, plate or a kind of false gold called pinchbeck were common, and some were intricately engraved and even set with precious stones. In 1765, a colonial gentleman noted in his diary, "Bought a gold stock buckle, £5.5.0.," and ten years later, *The Connoisseur* magazine reported, "The Beau Parson . . . his grizzle is scarcely orthodox . . . and is cropt behind to expose his diamond stock buckle."

By the 1730s, the stock had become generally popular, although its image still retained informal associations. Court mourning following the death of Frederick Prince of Wales in 1751 specified a cravat rather than a stock for this solemn and formal mode of dress. *The Gentleman's Magazine* reported, "The men to wear black cloth without buttons on the sleeves or pockets, plain muslin or long lawn cravats and weepers." However, when the 22-year-old, sporting George III ascended the British throne in 1760 and showed his preference for the stock, its triumph was temporarily assured.

Meanwhile, a coincidental development in hairstyles had led, in the 1730s, to the emergence of the solitaire — the descendant of 17th-century cravat strings.

Over the first few decades of the 18th century, wigs had diminished in size and had come to be characterized by a pigtail, which was sometimes contained in a small, black bag. The resulting wig was thus known as a "bag-wig". Those who could not afford a suitable one simply tied their hair back with a black ribbon, and many gentlemen who found wigs uncomfortable imitated them, especially in France and Italy. For those who ached to be in the forefront of fashion — and therefore felt compelled to wear the plain and simple stock — and yet longed for more adornment than a collar of white linen would allow, this broad black ribbon was a gift, and they seized on it with passion.

They brought its long ends round to the front of their necks and tied them in a bow over their stock. They tucked the ends into their shirt front or left the ends to dangle over their chest. They even pinned their ribbons to their shirt fronts — a style noted by Tobias Smollet in his novel *The Adventures of Roderick Random* (1748), when he comments on "a brooch set with garnets that glittered in the breast of his shirt."

Enterprising men felt that one solitaire — which took its name from its singular state — was not enough of a good thing. If one black ribbon was chic, then several brightly colored ribbons might be more so, and duly strung them round their necks. The arrangements eventually became so convoluted and ridiculous that the solitaire was a favorite target for satirists of the fashionable world, and the subject of much derision.

"A coxcomb wears a solitaire and uses paint," sneered Smollett in *The Expedition of Humphrey Clinker* (1771), linking the style to the emerging class of dandies who, as La Rochefoucauld observed in *Mélanges sur l'Angleterre*, "have their toilettes set out with washes, perfumes and cosmetics; and will spend a whole morning scenting their linen, dressing their hair, and arching their eyebrows."

Satirist Christopher Anstey was more subtle in his attack. Mr Simpkins, hero of Anstey's 1766 poem *The New Bath Guide*, writes to his mother: "But what with my Nivernois hat can compare/Bagwig and lac'd ruffles and black solitaire?/And what can a man of true fashion denote/Like an ell of good ribbon tied under the throat?" Even the popular gentlemen's magazines joined the chorus. A skit on the "man of fashion," carried by *The London Magazine, or Gentleman's Monthly Intelligencer* in 1764 waxed lyrical: "First let down a taper tail/Ty'd with ribbon to incline/Twirl by twirl, to spiral line . . . For his flowing solitaire."

The stock, too, was a subject for complaint. By 1761, after three decades of asphyxiation, a contributor to *The Gentleman's Magazine* was not ashamed to confess, "My neck is stretched out in such a manner that I am apprehensive of having my throat cut with the pasteboard." And an old gentleman in David Garrick's play *Bon Ton, or High Life above Stairs* (1775) attacks the style vehemently. "I wish that he who first changed long neckcloths for such things as you wear had the wearing of the twisted neckcloth that I would give him," he snorts to a young blood. This aged stalwart is observed to cling to the *passé* Steinkirk style — "One of the knots of his tie hanging down his left shoulder, and his fringed cravat nicely twisted down his breast and thrust thru' his gold buttonhole" — and although he was certainly behind the times, he was not alone in his preference.

The prevalence of such styles was not as great as a student of 18th-century painting might assume. Sitting for your portrait in clothes that would have been worn by your ancestors was highly fashionable, so Tudor doublets and Vandyke

Top: *Portrait of A Man* by **Rosalba Carriera, 1758. This painting shows the sitter wearing a plain white linen stock, wrapped tightly above a waistcoat.**

Above: *Portrait of Billaud-Varenne (1756–1819)* by **Jean-Baptiste Greuze (1725–1805). 1790. Billaud-Varenne wears a copious linen stock with a loose bow sewn on at the front.**

Above: *Portrait of Jacques Cazotte* (1719–92) by J.B. Perronneau (1715–83), *c*1763. Cazotte is wearing a simple broad black solitaire, a white linen or muslin stock and lace shirt frills.

Right: *Mariage à la Mode* (The Marriage Contract) by William Hogarth (1697–1764), 1743. In recording scenes of domestic drama, Hogarth was particularly aware of the potency of dress to convey character. The bridegroom's vanity is emphasized by his opulent blue coat and bowed solitaire.

collars were common anachronisms, while the Steinkirk persisted in art — and especially in provincial painting — long after it had ceased to be popular in real life. Artists such as Reynolds and Gainsborough encouraged this freak of fancy and second-rate or colonial painters are far more likely to have left an accurate portrayal of contemporary neckwear.

Sensible, active men had retained a few cravats in their wardrobes throughout the century, as one Parson Woodford revealed in his 1762 diary, when he listed nine shirts, nine stocks and two cravats. It is not known whether it was boredom after 50 years of stock-wearing, a sudden whim of a few fashion leaders, or a collective coming-to-the-senses of half-strangled men, but by the 1780s, the majority of Europeans had had enough of discomfort and began to revert to the cravat.

This "new" neckcloth took its name from its 17th-century predecessor, but it was a very different piece of clothing to the delicate, lacy confections that had adorned Louis XV, Charles II and James II. It consisted of a large square of muslin or lawn, folded first in a triangle and then refolded into a band, which was passed around the neck and knotted in a bow at the throat.

It was also simple to make at home, and hordes of dutiful mothers, daughters and sisters took up their needles to hem cravats for their menfolk — a development which did not please the tradesmen who had been doing a roaring trade in ready-to-wear stock collars and covers since the 1760s, when one observer noted, "It is now become an universal practice for taylors and drapers to make up their own goods," although these were not the most fashionable available. Jane Austen made her brothers' cravats, as did Catherine, the heroine of her novel *Northanger Abbey* (written in 1798–9 but published in 1818). It was not always the most reliable of manufacturing processes, as Catherine's mother complains when her daughter takes her time over her task: "Mama wailed, 'I do not know when poor Richard's cravats would be done, if he had no friend but you.'"

The first to favor the new, soft cravat style were the Macaronis, a group of fashionable young British society men who formed a club in 1764 to promote

**Left: Two men and a woman
by Joseph Wright of Derby
(1734–97). 1781–2. The men
wear the new soft cravats that
were less restrictive than the
asphyxiating stocks.**

the idea that male dress should be made simpler and plainer, less tight and restrictive at the neck and less prone to lavish embroidery and jewels below it. However, somehow, within a few years of the announcement of this philosophy, the movement was hijacked by men with exactly the opposite idea, those who longed to build on and exaggerate the extravagant styles favored in the previous century.

Lace at the throat and wrists, super-fine materials, jewels, buckles, scent and ribbons — the Macaroni's motto was "Everything in excess." By 1772 the very name was an insult used to describe the most absurd kind of fop or popinjay. That year, *The Town and Country Magazine* described a Macaroni in tones of the deepest disgust as a "most ridiculous figure . . . Such a figure, essenced and perfumed, with a bunch of lace sticking out under its chin, puzzles the common passenger to determine the thing's sex."

Lace wasn't the only cravat material favored by these extraordinary creatures. Some adopted a narrow, lace-edged length of muslin tied in a bow under the chin with long ends dangling over the chest. Others opted for silk and fringes, as *The Gentleman's and London Magazine* reported in 1777. "The silken ornament worn by way of cravat is of such importance to the taste, especially when the knot is elegantly fringed," it jeered.

The fame of the Macaronis spread fast and far — to America, where in 1775 patriots had begun their rebellion against their absentee landlord George III, his heavy taxes, and especially the Stamp Act.

The colonial soldiery wore "variegated, ill-fitting and incomplete" uniforms, and the British, wishing to take any advantage possible in a war which was deeply unpopular both at home and among other colonial powers, did not hesitate to stoop to cheap jibes in an effort to belittle their enemy. One such was the song "Yankee Doodle Dandy," written by a British soldier to aggravate the American troops. Unfortunately the joke backfired.

Yankee Doodle came to town,
Riding on a pony,
Stuck a feather in his hat
And called it Macaroni!

It sounded like patriotic gobbledygook to unsophisticated Americans, who took the song for their own and parroted it across the country, unaware of the insult implied.

Eventually the Americans added their own stanzas, attacking General Washington's aristocratic pretensions as observed during his visit to the Provincial Camp at Cambridge, Massachusetts. This version, beginning "Father and I went down to camp . . . " complains that Washington "got him on his meeting clothes," wears "flaming ribbons in his hat" and rides with "gentlefolks about him" and not with his troops. It was a fitting inversion of the original purpose of the song, and a fine demonstration of the new country's attitude to extravagant costume. What had begun as a satire meant to ridicule provincialism and vulgarity shown through clothing ended as a satire intended to ridicule aristocratic pretension, revealed in the same way.

That down-to-earth approach had showed throughout the century in the American attitude to neckwear. Although they were becoming better established and organized, the colonists had continued to lag well behind the fashionable times of Europe and Britain and to favor simple, practical styles above all. A long, plain cravat — made of a strip of lawn about 6 feet (1.8 m) long and wrapped twice around the neck, with the ends folded loosely over each other and left to hang on the chest — was popular from 1710 until the end of the Revolution, appearing most after 1729, by which time the stock was the fashionable neckwear of Europe. Lawn cravats were, for instance, advertised in the *Boston Post* in 1735.

Steinkirks, too, persisted, being taken up widely only from about 1729 and remaining in favor until the end of the 1740s. The ultra-fashionable and wealthy Governor Jonathan Belcher of Massachusetts was proud to be seen in his Steinkirk and lace ruffles as late as 1731, the year he took up his post. And a plain cravat, tucked into and slightly puffed over the waistcoat was a favorite from 1725 until the end of the century, although it was most popular during the years between 1750 and the Revolution.

Right: A portrait of Captain Samuel Chandler by Winthrop Chandler, 1780. American neckwear tended to be slightly less formal than its English counterpart for everyday wear, but formal attire necessitated imported linens. Chandler here wears a stock and narrow shirt frill.

Above: A gentleman wearing a plain, soft stock of fine white linen or muslin. Late 18th century.

Left: A portrait of Eustache-Ignace Trottier (known as des Rivieres) by Francois Beaucourt, 1793. Here a light bow is worn above shirt frills and a heavily embroidered waistcoat. The look is ostentatiously old-fashioned.

When the stock came to be worn by colonists, it never reached the ludicrous and unhealthy proportions favored by fashionable Europeans. Stocks appear in American portraits from around 1735 and were being advertised in newspapers such as the *Boston Post*, which offered "Stock-tapes . . . newest fashioned plaited stocks" in 1764. But they only became widely popular in the mid-1770s, by which time they were on the wane on the other side of the Atlantic. American men were conservative — and sensible — in their adoption of the new fashion, preferring a single pleated or folded wrap of white linen, sometimes stiffened, which ended comfortably under the chin, to the soaring monstrosities worn by the British bucks and beaux.

It was no wonder that the British, fighting their hopeless battles to keep control of the rich young country, found American clothing an easy target for satire. Comfort and practicality were not, after all, the hallmarks of a gentleman's dress: smartness was the thing. To make matters even worse, the Americans had the nerve to adopt what was, in Europe, an almost entirely working-class fashion — the type of handkerchief which we now know as the bandanna.

In the 18th century, a handkerchief was a larger, grander affair than the

Above: A street vendor from the *Cries of London* series by Paul Sandby. This character wears a bandanna, basically a square of fabric, folded and swathed loosely around the neck, then knotted in a bow at the throat. Nottingham Art Gallery.

small scrap of material we now use for nose blowing. That, at the time of the American Revolution, would have been called a "pocket handkerchief." To the vast majority of people then, a handkerchief was a large colored square, typically 2–3 feet (0.6–0.9 m) wide, folded diagonally and most often worn as a neckcloth by working-class men and women. But to the upper classes who would have provided the officers in George III's anti-revolutionary army, a handkerchief was a particularly ample pocket handkerchief favored by snuff-takers, and anybody who wore one around the neck was betraying plebeian origins. As far as they were concerned, soldiers wearing handkerchiefs were simply soldiers without proper uniforms and, by extension, without proper discipline. Real soldiers — efficient, well-drilled, professional British soldiers — wore military stocks. Despite this, such handkerchiefs were in great demand, and became the first widely available and distinct type of neckwear of the lower classes — one which would be seen in paintings and photographs until the 20th century.

The originals of the bandanna handkerchief, first brought to Europe early in the 18th century, were made from Indian silks in blue, red, green, brown, purple, yellow, pink, black and white, tie-dyed, or printed or handblocked in Bengal with birds'-eye spots, lozenges or flowers. They were exported first to Britain and Holland by the English and Dutch East India companies and then to the rest of Europe and the colonies.

Initially, these textiles were known as *rumals* (also spelled *romal* or *roomaul*) or *taffa de foolas*. But as the power of the English East India Company grew, the name *bandanna* (alternatively *bandannoe* or *bandana*) — a corruption of the Sanskrit word *bandhna* (or *bandhana*) meaning "tying" — was adopted as the generic description.

The fact that, in Britain, bandannas were prohibited goods, under the Calico Acts of 1700 and 1720, only added to their attraction. They were supposed to be sold purely for export, via the East India Company's salerooms in London, but were often re-imported into England via Holland, Germany, Belgium and the Channel Islands and were resold for between two and eight shillings each — roughly twice their original price. By the 1750s, hundreds of thousands of bandannas were finding their way into England and America, and so much money was to be made that British manufacturers began to copy the Indian goods in cotton and linen as well as silk, before perfecting the techniques in the 1770s. They became a specialty of the textile-printing trade of Manchester.

The bandanna had a number of attractions for working-class Europeans. A neckcloth was a mark of respectability, but the cravats and stocks available were too expensive for a working man's pocket, and the discomfort and laundering they required were impractical for his lifestyle. A bandanna, on the other hand, was brightly colored and patterned and therefore did not show the dirt, and when necessary it was easily washable. It was a major expense, true, but when you only needed a couple and acquired instant status by wearing one, a few shillings was a small price to pay. What was more, it was multifunctional. Not only could it be knotted around the neck; it could also be used instead of a basket, as a lead for animals, for mopping a sweating brow or for brightening up the brim of a hat.

By the 1740s, the Americans were also clamoring for bandannas, and a thriving trade built up between Britain and the Atlantic seaboard, especially in the South. The colonists were not only less fashion conscious than their European cousins; they were also less class conscious, and saw the advantages of a practical, comfortable form of neckwear that the English would have considered them-selves too middle class — or in too formal a situation, such as an army at war — to be seen wearing rather than a stock or cravat.

So farmers, foremen and senior servants were quick to place orders for rumals

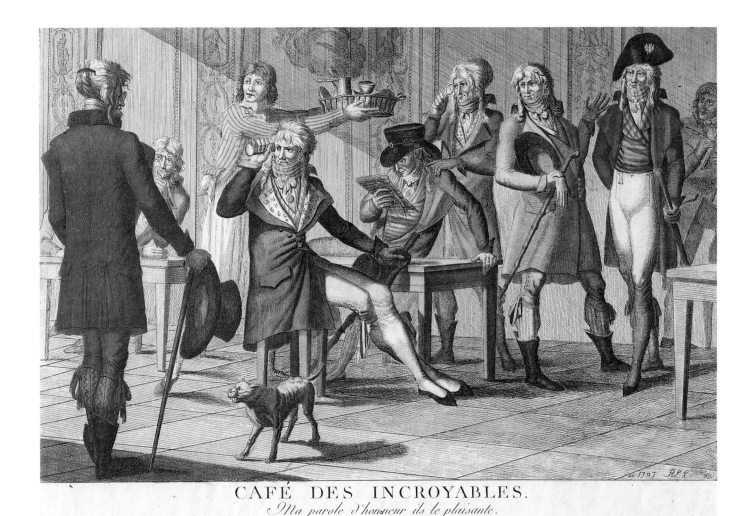

CAFÉ DES INCROYABLES.

Ma parole d'honneur ils le plaisante.

and bandannas. Tied loosely around the neck with the knot at the throat, these kerchiefs were the perfect neckwear for informal rides, visits to the fields to check on workers, and other active tasks. A description written for the *Old Colony Memorial* in 1820 describes the dress of such middle-class men in rural areas at the time of the Revolution. "They had flannel shirts and stockings and thick leather shoes," it states. "A silk handkerchief would last for ten years."

In America, too, the trade in silk kerchiefs was highly competitive. The *South Carolina Gazette* of May 28, 1752, for example, records a number of advertisements for this new neckwear. "James Laurens and Comp . . . Imported in the Industry, Pearson, from London and the Hereford, Peard, from Bristol and will sell at the most reasonable prices at their store on the Bay — a great variety of . . . bandannoes," reads one. A competing firm promises, "Just imported in the Fortrose, Capt Mackenzie, and in the Industry, Capt Pearson . . . bandannoes . . . to be sold at the store in Broad Street lately possessed by messrs Alexander Cramahe and Company."

Charleston, South Carolina, has also yielded the sole examples of 18th-century Bengal bandannas so far discovered in an archeological context in the United States. When the old Exchange Building on the waterfront was excavated in 1980, fragments of bandannas, buried by the great hurricane of September 14, 1752, were found.

Records of the new neckwear in America are, however, sparse. A naive painting of the Delaware or Pennsylvania school, *circa* 1775, shows one Israel Israel with a light-colored spotted kerchief; the merchant James Beekman of New

Above: *Café des Incroyables* by Gravano, *c*1795–1799. Directoire neckwear as worn by the Incroyables or Unbelievables. The bandaged effect was achieved by many yards of muslin, often patterned, being wrapped repeatedly around the neck, supporting the chin and sometimes covering it. Musée du Carnavalet, Paris.

Right: James Belcher by an unknown artist, late 18th century. The sitter, a famous pugilist, is shown here wearing a bandanna, a popular form of neckwear among large numbers of Americans from all classes. It was favored for its practicality and comfort. This is a particularly fine example in a patterned material. The neckcloth Belcher made famous was dark blue spotted with white or light blue birdseyes.

York ordered "spotted red Bandanna" kerchiefs for himself in 1773; and the painting *Brook Watson and the Shark* by J. S. Copley (1778) shows American seamen wearing bandanna neckcloths as they man the oars of a boat into which the 14-year-old Brook Watson — who has just lost a leg to a shark — is about to be hauled from the waters of Havana Harbor. Other paintings of the time tend to show working men wearing idealized versions of city neckcloths, and Doriece Colle suggests, in her book *Collars, Stocks, Cravats*, that "Sunday" neckwear imitating gentrified styles was made from scraps of material by even the poorest citizens.

Still, it seems clear from the huge numbers of bandannas and kerchiefs imported, from the names of the prosperous men who bought them, and from the unfussy, common-sense approach to fashion adopted by even the grandest Americans, that the bandanna was a common form of neckwear in the young country.

The wide swathe of Americans who wore their bandannas simply because they were suitable and sensible would probably have snorted in disgust had they been told that they were in the forefront of fashion — indeed, they were the first middle-class men to wear the colored neckwear that would become the norm in the next century. But Europe did catch up, although it would be the turn of the century before the majority of men would feel comfortable in such neckwear.

Perhaps it was a euphoric response to the freedoms promised by the American and French Revolutions, but throughout the 1780s and 1790s some extraordinarily flamboyant cravats became popular. The most remarkable was the *Incroyable* neckcloth favored by the nonconformists who were known as the Incroyables — literally, the Unbelievables — throughout Europe during the years when the Directory ruled France. Yards of white linen or muslin were wrapped around the neck, the chin and even the face so that the wearer looked as if he might have a bad toothache or the mumps, and vast floppy bows drooped across the shoulders. In extreme cases, two sheets of muslin were used, one black and one white, to advertise Republican sympathies, and create an even more bizarre effect.

These strange cravats, of "an almost incredible size," are satirized by H. Le Blanc in his *The Art of Tying the Cravat*. "By this *echafaudage* the neck was placed on a level with the head, which in size it surpassed, and with which it was confounded," he writes.

Above: A self-portrait by J.M.W. Turner (1775–1851), *c*1798. In this early painting, the young Turner wears a cravat of white linen wrapped to just beneath the chin and tied at the front.

> The shirt collar rose to the sides of the ears, and the top of the cravat covered the mouth and the lower part of the nose, so that the face (with the exception of the nose) was concealed by the cravat and a forest of whiskers; these rose on each side of the hair, which was combed down over the eyes. In this costume the *elegans* bore a greater resemblance to beasts than men, and the fashion gave rise to many laughable caricatures. They were compelled to look straight before them, as the head could only be turned by the general consent of all the members, and the *tout ensemble* was that of an unfinished statue.

At the same time, French Royalists who wanted to flaunt their allegiance wore green neckcloths, or stuck to loosely circling ribbons, low stocks or stocks with solitaires.

The British – who had not faced the horrors suffered across the Channel and had not fully realized that Madame Guillotine had sliced away forever lace

NECKCLOTHS AND THE NOOSE

In the course of the 18th century, the fact that neckwear was so rigid that it might well strangle a man had become enshrined in popular slang. "Neckcloth" — or "neckinger", "necksqueezer" or "necktie" — had become synonymous with "halter" or "noose". And in the early years of the 19th century, the term was even featured in a British cant song, "The Night Before Larry Was Stretched," in which the condemned man declares, "For the neckcloth I don't care a button."

The association persisted and was common in America. In 1877, J. H. Beadle wrote in *Western Wilds*, "He joined the Vigilantes, and had the pleasure of presiding at a necktie sociable where two of the men who had robbed him were hanged."

THE BANDANNA SMUGGLERS

Fortunes were made and lost, and thievery and skullduggery of all kinds were practiced, in the pursuit of the lucrative bandanna trade in England.

A report to the House of Commons of 1745 commemorates the capture of some unsuccessful smugglers by customs officers from Yarmouth on the east coast, giving some idea of the scale of the market.

> On the 22nd October, one hundred and twelve horses were laden on the beach near Benacre with dry goods [the classification for Indian silks at the time] by upwards of ninety men, guarded by ten persons with firearms. And on the 20th of the same month forty horses were laden with dry goods at Kartley by riders well armed.

The kerchiefs were smuggled into the country in continuous lengths, then cut and resold, legally, as single bandannas. So those buying bandannas in the shops were in no danger of prosecution.

Above: A self-portrait by Louis Léopold Boilly, *c*1800. The painter is wearing a length of white linen or muslin wrapped around his neck tie into a knot just under his chin.

Opposite: A self-portrait by Jacques-Louis David (1748–1825). The revolutionary artist wears a flamboyant but not ridiculous neckcloth – an almost *croyable* "incroyable".

bows and ruffles along with aristocratic heads — were more conservative. Some groups of faddish young men about town — the likes of the Jessamys, Jeremys, Smarts, Dappers and Sparks as well as the latter-day Macaronis — did take up more extreme styles, and were parodied for doing so. But the majority of men progressed to the modified soft cravat, described in October 1788 by the *Ipswich Journal* as "A large muslin cravat [wrapped] three times round the neck, the ends of which are trimmed with a fine deep lace edging and tied in a large knot under the chin."

Even this was not a great advance in comfort, as the material was wrapped high around the neck. The author of the *Torrington Diaries* wrote in 1789 of his relief at freeing himself from its restrictions. "At last home I come, clap on my bedgown, my slippers, take off my gaiters, ease my neckcloth," he confided. The sigh of relief is almost audible across the centuries.

From here, it was only a short step to the strict manliness and purity of line later perfected by the great Beau Brummell. But *en route*, men came to accept the idea of colored and patterned bandanna neckcloths so popular among Americans. Toward the end of the 18th century, Jem Belcher, the pugilist, was much admired by the young bucks and bloods. One of his personal quirks — perhaps the result of his rise from his working-class beginnings — was to wear a blue silk bandanna, decorated with large white spots with pale blue birds'-eye centers, as a high cravat. Fashionable young men soon copied their idol, and before long, the Belcher neckcloth was widely acceptable at informal and sporting events. Belcher also gave his name to the earliest known scarf ring: a thick, plain band of gold through which his bandanna was pulled before being puffed up and folded across the throat and secured over the upper chest, obscuring the ring.

The adoption of the Belcher neckcloth was a turning point in male fashion. It was essentially working class in origin, practical, colorful and easy to tie. It was a bridge between working-class and American pragmatism and middle- and upper-class formality. And although Brummell was soon to lay the foundations for the British look, which has dominated menswear ever since the early 19th century, Belcher was the man who popularized the first truly modern necktie, the spiritual ancestor of those seen in every office and men's clothing store today.

. . . AND NOWHERE TO GO

It was hardly surprising that Americans lagged behind Europeans in the invention and popularizing of new fashions. Even if materials had been available, the vast majority of the colonists had nowhere to show them off.

There was an imitation "court" in late 18th-century Boston, which Nathaniel Hawthorne would later describe in somewhat disapproving terms. "There are tokens everywhere of a style of luxury and magnificence we had not associated with our notions of the times," he wrote about the balls, assemblies, horse races and regattas which took place. However, even in such circles, styles such as the solitaire were only appearing at the time of the Revolution.

These lavish excitements were reserved for provincial governors and their friends. Most

Americans had to content themselves with spinning matches, singing schools, single-sex gatherings and the occasional dance — held, perhaps, in honor of the birth of a royal baby (before the Revolution), or to celebrate a good harvest.

It was with a sharp eye to these honest, decent folk and their priorities that George Washington — despite his own pretenses to dandyism — penned his nephew a now-famous letter containing advice on the clothing suitable to a man in the newly independent America. "Do not conceive that fine clothes make fine men any more than fine feathers make fine birds," he wrote on January 15, 1783. "A plain genteel dress is more admired and obtains more credit than lace and embroidery in the eyes of the sensible."

Brummell and the Dandies: 1800–1830

Above: An advertisement for Beau Brummel Ties Inc. Cincinnati, 1948. The enduring influence of Beau Brummel lead to manufacturers exploiting his name even into the 20th century. Here ties with abstract patterns are promoted – though they bear no resemblance to the ties Brummel would have worn.

By the end of the 18th century, all the old certainties had been shaken to their foundations. After the revolutions in America and, more importantly, France, the upper classes were no longer sure that they were superior, that breeding and education counted, that being a gentleman was what mattered most. There was fear and dislike of the vast and physically strong working class, fear and dislike of the growing and economically strong middle class and, above all, fear that exhibiting old aristocratic money and style would attract rather more than dislike from these two powerful groups.

A generation of Haves who had seen what the supposed Have-Nots could do when they were angry became confused about the best way to behave, the right way to project themselves, even the correct way to dress. What, in the aftermath of revolution, was a gentleman? How did one recognize a superior human being? It was obviously no longer sensible to flaunt one's wealth by wearing it in the form of lace, satin and brocade – so what was a man to wear?

For the bewildered souls of the early 19th century, George Bryan Brummell (1778–1840) had the answers.

He was a gentleman because he looked like one. He was superior because he looked better than anybody else. And as for costume — why, any man who wished to show himself to the best advantage had merely to follow Brummell's example and adopt clothes of the most extreme simplicity, the most exquisite cut and the most scrupulous cleanliness.

The Brummell philosophy was to change menswear forever and his principles guide what men wear even today.

His outfit consisted of a tight tailcoat, with the lapels rising to the ears and revealing a line of waistcoat and the folds of the cravat, with comfortable pantaloons tucked into glossy knee boots — nothing more, nothing less. The clothes should be somber, form-fitting but not restricting, severely plain and indubitably masculine. Even the colors were laid down: blue for the coat, buff for the waistcoat and pantaloons, black for the boots and the brightest, cleanest white for the cravat.

As Brummell's earliest and most effusive biographer, Captain Jesse, pointed out, "His chief aim was to avoid anything marked." In other words, a gentleman was to be known by his discretion, his lack of vulgar show. Only in the arrangement of his cravat was a man of fashion permitted to show any individuality or suggest his personal whims and tastes. The cult of the neckcloth had begun.

In retrospect, Brummell's solution seems obvious, but at the time it was seen as inspired and he was hailed as a genius. The Have-Nots and the rising middle classes could afford their own version of such an outfit and enjoy high fashion for the first time, while the Haves could lavish their money on the very best tailoring, the crispest laundering and the attentions of valets who would help them to confect a neckcloth which anybody could see had taken considerable skill and time to arrange.

Even Brummell's own parentage underlined the democratic nature of such a costume. He made a point of stressing his humble lineage, claiming, tongue in cheek, "My father was a very superior valet," although he had been, in fact, a senior civil servant who sent his son to Eton and Oxford University and left him a substantial inheritance of at least £15,000 — a fabulous sum at the time.

Brummell was of sturdy middle-class stock and not an aristocrat — "A nobody who made himself somebody, and gave the law to everybody," as one contemporary remarked tartly. Brummell gave all men a goal as well as a uniform — if he could reach the pinnacle of society, then anybody could, providing he had the

Below: Further examples of ties from the Beau Brummel Company. These casual South Pacific prints are here recommended as the ideal present.

Left: Portrait of Beau Brummel by J. Cook, after a miniature, 1844. The doyen of dandies, Beau Brummel laid the foundation for a British style of rigidly simple menswear that persists today. He is shown wearing a distinctive high neckcloth. National Portrait Gallery, London.

Below: "These, Sir, are our failures."
In an effort to arrive at Brumwellian
perfection of the cravat, men around
the world tore, crumpled and stained
dozens of neckcloths every morning.
This man's valet clearly thinks his
master is an idiot to try to ape his idol.

Below: George IV from Jesse's *Life of
Brummel*, wearing a Royal George.

same determination and the same exquisite taste.

The Beau's climb to prominence began when, while serving with the Tenth Hussars shortly after leaving Oxford, he became a friend of "Prinny," the Prince of Wales, who later became the Prince Regent and later still George IV. The Tenth Hussars were known at the time as "The Elegant Extracts" and "The Prince's Own Command," and the plump, dandified prince — whose entire claim to sartorial fame lay in his invention of a ludicrous shoe buckle, 1 inch by 5 inches (2.5 cm by 12. 5 cm) — was fascinated by the insouciant chic of his cool young officer. By the time young Brummell had resigned his commission in 1798 and took up residence in a small London townhouse, Prinny was captivated and longed to emulate his friend.

And the thing that he — like every other society figure of the day — most longed to emulate was the perfection of Brummell's neckcloth. Once he arrived to watch and study his friend at his morning toilet. The process took so long that the Prince was obliged to send his horses away and ask Brummell to give him a quiet dinner.

Brummell's great secret was actually quite simple. "Fine linen, plenty of it, and country washing," was how he put it himself. More simply, the Beau insisted on using ample, lightly starched cravats which he spent as long as was necessary to knot, fold, pleat and arrange to perfection.

He would never have dreamed of reusing a grubby or crumpled piece of linen, and often changed his neckcloth three times a day — a habit immortalized in an anecdote which circulated the London clubs of the time and is still recalled today. Apparently, callers one morning surprised Brummell's valet coming down the stairs with an armful of crumpled linen. The visitors seized their chance to satisfy their curiosity. What, they asked, was all this cloth, and how had it accumulated? The valet drew himself up and shrugged with sad dignity. "These," he said, "are our failures."

The important extra ingredient introduced by Brummell to the simple square of folded cambric, lawn, muslin or silk was starch. However, it had to be a light starch, so that the cravat could be arranged exactly, would hold its shape, and could be pressed into its final folds by a neat downward movement of the chin, without being so rigid that it would be uncomfortable or prevent the free movement of his head and neck. "In the rigid perfection of his linen," wrote Sir Max Beerbohm at the end of the century, "lay the secret of Mr Brummell's miracles."

Inevitably, anxious imitators took the Brummell cravat to extremes — something which amused the great man hugely. One night he was dining at the gentleman's club, Wattier's, when he spotted the young Marquis of Worcester, who had committed the cardinal sin of overstarching his cravat and could barely roll his eyes as a result.

"Is Lord Worcester here?" Brummell asked the waiter, although he could see the embarrassed peer sitting a mere two seats away.

"Yes, sir," replied the dutiful waiter.

"Tell his Lordship I would be happy to drink a glass of wine with him."

"Yes, sir," said the waiter, scurrying round into Worcester's field of vision and repeating the invitation.

"Is his Lordship ready?" Brummell inquired finally.

"Yes, sir," said the waiter after a last-minute check.

"Then tell him I drink his health!" said Brummell, permitting himself a wry smile.

Other dandies attempted to rival the great Beau: King Allen, whose entire daily exercise consisted of a walk between White's and another gentlemen's club, Crockford's; Silent Hare, who talked all the time; Pea-Green Hayne and

Blue-Hanger Lord Coleraine who each only wore one color; Teapot Crawford, named after an old black pot he had treasured since his schooldays at Eton; Romeo Coates, who acted in Shakespeare; Poodle Byng, who had tightly curled hair; and the fabulously wealthy Golden Ball Hughes.

Even the loss of Prinny's close friendship and patronage, which occurred when he became Regent in 1811, did not diminish Brummell's power over the fashionable world. He continued to reign from a seat as sacrosanct as any throne, in the bow window of the most exclusive of Regency gentlemen's clubs, White's. From this lookout, he would — according to the fashionable poet Henry Luttrell — pass judgment on unfortunate passers-by, "Whose cape's an inch too low or high;/Whose doctrines are unsound in hat,/In boots, in trowsers or cravat . . . "

Another satirical poem commemorated Brummell's obsession with the arrangement of his own neckwear:

My neckcloth, of course, forms my principal care,
For by that we criterions of elegance swear,
And costs me, each morning, some hours of flurry,
To make it appear to be tied in a hurry.

Under Brummell's influence, the finely arranged cravat gradually became the sign of the truly fashionable man. The rest of the costume could be contrived on a man's behalf by his tailor, but only he could manipulate the cravat itself into anything approaching perfection. How high this insignificant piece of linen had risen in the list of Regency priorities can be seen in Luttrell's table of contents for his *Advice to Julia*:

> Hyde Park – The Ride – The Promenade – The Opera – Newmarket – News of the Day – Sketch of a Small-Talker – The Park on Sundays – A Submissive Lover – The Mysteries of Dress – Importance of the Cravat . . .

This passion for fashionable neckwear did not spring entirely from the social insecurities of a large group of men with too much money and too little to do. After the French Revolution had come the Napoleonic wars, and the men who devoted so much time to their appearance were making a flippant and arrogant comment on the ambitions of the little Corsican who was attempting to take over the world. The hours of labor it took to achieve the perfect cravat might be seen by some as a ridiculous waste of time, but its subliminal message was that Boney's depredations on Europe could not prevent the English gentleman from concentrating on all the little things that made him so superior to his French counterpart.

It was a stance that even found its place on the field of battle, as Captain Gronow, one of Wellington's officers, recorded in a series of writings which chronicled the wars mainly from a sartorial standpoint. Gronow (who later settled in Paris and observed French dandies imitating their more creative British counterparts) remembered the Duke of Wellington — nicknamed "The Dandy" by his own troops during the Peninsular campaign — directing a defensive

Opposite: Young man by an unknown artist, *c*1800. Though drawn in a neo-classical style, this immaculately dressed figure wears contemporary costume including a high cravat to which he draws attention with his artificial pose.

THE SARTORIAL NAPOLEON

While the British aristocracy were dressing ever more simply and discreetly, the new Emperor Napoleon was determined to cover his court with glory, ruffles and frills.

His coronation, at which he wore an anachronistic lace jabot, cost four million francs, and new court uniforms were devised at the same time. Along with silver-embroidered coats, whose base color indicated a man's rank, went velvet cloaks, sashes, a hat adorned with a white plume and the bizarre combination of a 16th-century ruff worn with a drooping cravat.

Napoleon himself was something of a dandy, allotting himself a clothing allowance of 40,000 francs a year. He also insisted that the Imperial wardrobe should send clean neckwear and shirts to numerous potential pick-up points while he was on campaign so that he should never be without fresh linen.

Right: *Napoleon in Court Robes* by François Gerard (1770–1837). Napoleon is here seen in full ceremonial attire including an old-fashioned gold lace cravat.

engagement dressed in a gray greatcoat with a cape, a white cravat (its fashionableness unusual as most military men dressed uniformly in black stocks), Hessian boots, leather pantaloons and a large cocked hat *á la Russe*. The great Duke himself, who was only 46 when the wars finally ended in 1815 after Napoleon's defeat at Waterloo, was in the habit of pointing out that "the history of a battle is not unlike the history of a ball."

The doomed Napoleon decided to try out Wellington's dandified neckwear in his last days as emperor — but the switch from conventional black stock to fashionable white cravat proved unlucky for him. The Emperor normally wore black silk, "as was remarked as Wagram, Lodi, Marengo, Austerlitz and co.," reports H. Le Blanc. "But at Waterloo it was observed that, contrary to his usual custom, he wore a white handkerchief, with a flowing bow, although the day previous he appeared in his black Cravat."

Against this background, where fashion in general and the right neckcloth in particular had a moral and political significance, even Lord Byron's apparently facile list of the qualities which made a man somebody in the Regency takes on a different perspective. As well as wealth, talent and family, Byron mentioned, "Fashion, which indeed's the best/Recommendation; and to be well drest/Will very often supersede the rest."

With the end of the Napoleonic wars and the approach of the Prince Regent's accession to the throne came the end of Brummell's reign. One night in May 1816, he dined at his club as usual, then slipped into a post-chaise and fled over the Channel to France, where he escaped his debtors to become a tourist attraction, first in Calais, then in Caen, until he died in 1840, a senile old man looked after by charitable nuns.

Some 80 years after his ignoble exit from his native land, Sir Max Beerbohm acclaimed Brummell as the "father of modern costume," who had invented a way of dressing "so quiet, so reasonable, and, I say emphatically, so beautiful [that] at

Below: *Monstrosities* **of 1819 and 1820 by George Cruikshank, 1820. Fashion victims as satirized by the greatest caricaturist of the day. The high collars and cravats almost obscure the wearers' faces.**

VARIATIONS

White linen might be the traditional material for a follower of the great Brummell, but even the purist Le Blanc concedes that, after the Beau's flight to France, some variations were permissible — and shows that even the classic Regency man about town did not invariably wrap his neck in snowy material.

For the *cravate à l'Americaine*, for instance, "the prevailing color is sea green"; the *cravate mathematique* was seen in black taffeta or Levantine [a heavy silk]; the *cravate Irlandaise* and the *cravate à la Russe* could be worn in any preferred color; the *cravate casse coeur* was a vivid scarlet, and the *cravate à la gastronome* could be "a handkerchief of any kind," being an up-market version of the bandanna, "seldom worn prior to the age of 40, but this depends greatly on climate and constitution."

Starch, too, was not an essential for the Beau of the 1820s. The much-despised *cravate collier de cheval* and *cravate en cascade*, the Byron, the *cravate Irlandaise*, the *cravate à la Marathe*, the *cravate à la gastronome* and the *cravate à la paresseuse* were all soft and starch-free, hinting at the draped styles which were to follow in the 1830s.

Right: Man checking his appearance in a mirror, *Journal des Dames et des Modes*, Paris. This figure wears a colored cravat, the main point of interest in an otherwise monochrome outfit.

every step in the process of democracy these precepts will be strengthened."

Not every man, of course, could keep up with the Brummellian ideal, and contemporary sneers about those who got it wrong were common. "We met John looking quite hideous with his hair in powder, a pink neckcloth, blue waistcoat, nankin inexpressibles and blue coat," the *Wynne Diaries* recorded in 1805. Sarah, Lady Lyttleton, was even more slighting when she described a man she had seen at a wedding in 1808 as "A country coxcomb arrayed in all manner of brilliant colours with the most regular Brutus head-dress and the highest neckcloth and lee boards I ever beheld, stiffer than a poker."

Their time was to come. In the aftermath of Brummell's flight, male fashion — and the cult of the cravat in particular — entered one of its craziest, least reasonable periods.

Perhaps it was relief that the shadow of Napoleon had been banished which led to the extraordinary excrescences parodied by the cartoonist George Cruikshank in his two series *Monstrosities* and *London Dandies*. He showed rigid figures with spindly legs, pointed toes, puffed bosoms and ridiculously elongated necks, topped by heads which could not or would not turn because of the swathes of linen which bound them.

Brummell's tall, straight, close-fitting collar became the collar *à la guillotine*, held 2 inches (5 cm) away from the neck and climbing up over the ears with the help of whalebone stiffeners. His crisp but manageable cravat in lightly starched folds became a mountain range of stiff white cloth which choked the neck or, like a *yashmak*, concealed the face up to the nose. The effect was so much like a pillory that in the poem "The Fudge Family" (1818), it was suggested "That seats like our music stools soon must be found 'em/To twirl when the creatures may wish to look round 'em."

Any young man with pretensions, and any group who wished to be fashionable, joined the fun by inventing their own special cravat styles. Young sportsmen also competed to create the least imitable neckwear. Those who had formed clubs to celebrate their passion for driving horses at breakneck speed bequeathed cravats named after their organizations — the Whip, the Barouche, the Defiance, the Tandem and the Four-in-Hand, which ultimately gave its name to the style of necktie almost every man now wears.

"*La mode chez eux,*" said Stendhal after a visit to Britain, "*n'est pas un plaisir, mais un devoir.*" To help in this duty (interestingly, the word also means "homework") came the first necktie manual. *Neckclothitania* was published anonymously in 1818, and detailed 12 of the most popular styles, showing how to tie them and illustrating them clearly. It was a considerable success, but was later overshadowed by the works published in France, Italy and England as *The Art of Tying the Cravat*, written, it seems, by a variety of different authors.

Meanwhile, the French were catching on. After the defeat of Napoleon, anybody who was anybody in France was an anglophile, and the dandified styles which had once had a social significance in their home country became a fashion joke — albeit a popular one — abroad. Soon a certain Stefano Demarelli was giving Parisians private lessons in how to tie their cravats, a network of valets were charging handsomely for detailed information on their latest confections, and one Dr Véron, founder of the *Revue de Paris*, was wearing such extraordinary neckcloths that his friends addressed letters to him as "*À Monsieur Véron, dans sa cravate, Paris.*"

Right: Fashionables. A monstrous caricature showing men in cheek- and even eye-level collars with gross cravats.

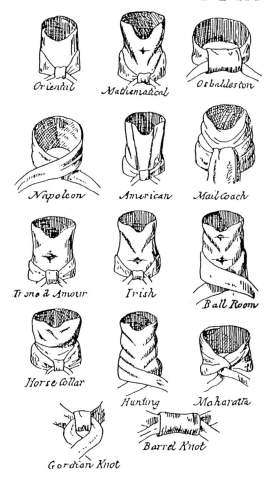

NECKCLOTHITANIA

Oriental — Mathematical — Oʃbaldeʃton
Napoleon — American — Mail Coach
Trone d'Amour — Irish — Ball Room
Horse Collar — Hunting — Maharatta
Gordian Knot — Barrel Knot

1 8 1 8

By the 1820s, cravat mania had swept Europe – and generated the first international bestseller, *L'Art de se mettre la cravate*, published in 1827, apparently written by a Baron Emile de l'Empesé. It contained a history of neckwear, all manner of social observation on the importance of the cravat, explicit instructions on the tying of 32 styles, and meticulous illustrations to help the bewildered male differentiate between such cravats as *l'Américaine, l'Orientale*, the Byron, the *collier de cheval* and the *cravate en cascade*.

Later that year, a similar book written by a Conte della Salda appeared in Italy. It, too, contained a history of neckwear, social observations, detailed instructions and meticulous illustrations of such cravats as *l'Américaine, l'Orientale*, the Byron . . . So did a book which was published in London in 1828 under the title, *The Art of Tying the Cravat*, by H. Le Blanc.

For some years, it was generally believed that this spate of sartorial literature was merely the coincidental result of three separate authors taking advantage of widespread neckcloth mania — the sort of nonsense satirized by Henry Luttrell in another of his telling verses:

All is unprofitable, flat,
And stale, without a smart CRAVAT;
Muslin'd enough to hold its starch —
That last keystone of Fashion's arch.

London Publish'd by W.S. Fores 50 Piccadilly Aug.t 9th 1817

O_d Angelic pon honor—fascinating Creature monstrous handsome!! D_m me if she isn't Divinity!! for further particulars enquire of the Original.

But the texts of the books are almost identical, except for a few asides suitable for each national identity; and the names of the authors, who never appeared in public to capitalize on their great success, translate, respectively, as Baron Starch, Count Starched and H. White or Starch! Clearly, these cravat books were written by a man with a great sense of humor, and the admonitions and anecdotes they contain should be viewed with a reasonable amount of skepticism.

The most popular candidate for their authorship has long been Honoré de Balzac, whose own printing house published the original book. Some have suggested that he wrote the books to settle his debts with various shirtmakers and drapers, and the long list of suitable tradesmen at the back of the French edition does support this theory. However, Balzac's first known pieces of professional writing were only produced around the time that *L'Art de se mettre la cravate* was published, and although one of his earliest pieces of journalism was entitled *"Physiologie de la toilette: De la cravate considérée en elle-meme et dans ses rapports avec le société . . . ,"* it was published in 1830 and postdates the L'Empesé/Della Salda/Le Blanc books by several years.

Whoever lurked behind the pseudonyms, he chronicled neckcloth mania with great success and parodied the obsession so subtly that several apocryphal stories have passed into history as genuine fact. Separating truth from fiction within these books isn't always easy, but one clearly teasing story concerns a soldier whose neckcloth had apparently stopped a bullet and saved his life.

In the English version, Le Blanc relates the tale as told to him by one Doctor Pizis, who had always laughed at a General Lepale "on account of his enormous cravat." Both these names are jokes in themselves, since Pizis is a corruption of *pisser*, "to pass water" and, colloquially "to make a fool of an unsuspecting person," and Lepale again means "white" and, by extension, "well-scrubbed and starched."

Le Blanc quotes Pizis as saying,

> I was informed that the General had been struck by a pistol shot in the throat. I immediately hastened to his assistance, and was shewn a bullet, which was stopped in its career by the very Cravat I had just been ridiculing. — Two officers and several privates had received sabre cuts on the cravat, and escaped without injury; so that I was obliged to confess that these immense bandages were not always useless.

Another obvious joke is the stern warning: "The greatest insult that can be offered to a man, *comme il faut*, is to seize him by the Cravat; in this case, blood only [that is, a duel or fight] can wash out the stain upon the honour of either party." Certainly, some young men of fashion did take their appearances this seriously at the time, but most people would have thought them downright silly. Le Blanc must have laughed uproariously at the thought.

A third joke lurks in the description of the *cravate à l'Americaine*, a genuine style of the day which may have been invented by a rare American dandy but was more probably thought up in Europe and named as a tribute to the young country, since although it is predictably "easily formed," Le Blanc describes it as being most uncomfortable.

> [Among] our friends, the fashionables of the New World, [who] pride themselves on its name, which they call "Independence"; this title may, to a certain point, be disputed, as the neck is fixed in a kind of vice, which entirely prohibits any very free movements,

says the author, who then goes on to double the jest by asserting that one of the favored color schemes for this cravat is stripes of red, white and blue. Even the

Opposite: "D-d Angelic pon honour – fascinating Creature . . . monstrous handsome!! D-m me if she isn't a Divinity!!". Etching by George Cruikshank, 1817. Victoria and Albert Museum, London.

word "fashionables" can be read as an implied insult which cultured Europeans would enjoy. Americans were not, as yet, a fashionable nation – but nor were they in the habit of inventing garish, uncomfortable neckwear.

However, Le Blanc and his alter egos were not entirely flippant when they penned the thesis which justified their pamphlets:

> The Cravat should not be considered a mere ornament, it is decidedly one of the greatest preservatives of health — it is a criterion by which the rank of the wearer may be at once distinguished, and it is of itself "a letter of introduction."

They had targeted the crucial point about the cravat within the new post-Brummell male costume. Man is by nature hierarchical, and even when his choice of clothing is restricted by a set formula, he will always find a way of showing his status and individuality. Since Brummell, the cravat or tie has offered the best — and, for conventional men, the only — opportunity for this self-expression.

With such a profusion of styles, some of them ludicrous, it's hardly surprising that Le Blanc, bearing in mind Brummell's dictum that nothing in a gentleman's costume should be "too marked," should caution against the effect of more extreme and relaxed fashions:

Right: Ludwig Van Beethoven (1770–1827) by Schinon. An artist of his standing could afford to be a little relaxed in his cravat, which is lower and looser than was strictly fashionable. Nobody would have worried too much about whether the composer was a gentleman – he was a genius, which was enough. Hans Beethoven, Bonn.

GH Harlow del. **Lord Byron**

**Left: Lord Byron (1788–1824),
an engraving by G.H. Harlow.
Byron rarely wore a neckcloth
or tie of any kind and is shown
in an open-necked shirt with a
large soft collar. A multiplicity
of ties were however named
after him in the course of the
19th century.**

Coloured handkerchiefs should be as plain as possible; we must, however, give it as our opinion, that they can only be worn *en déshabillé* at home, or when going to bathe, ride &c., early in the morning.

Likewise some styles are singled out as vulgar and pretentious. The *collier de cheval*, for instance, is stigmatized. "It has been greatly admired by the fair sex, who have praised it to their husbands, their lovers, and even to their friends and relations," says Le Blanc," and have thus promoted it by every means in their power." But he concludes, "This style is rather vulgar, and we have introduced it here, more that it may be avoided as an instance of false taste, than as a model or copy."

The Byron — at that time a big, floppy bow in brown, black or white — was another neckcloth which should not be seen in formal circumstances although Le Blanc suggests that it is "extremely comfortable in summer time, and during long journeys." "As Lord Byron differed so widely from the world in general, we can hardly expect to find in the Cravat worn by this prince of poets any of that elegance *recherchée* which generally characterises an Englishman of rank," he warns, ignoring the fact that Byron himself almost never wore a neckcloth or tie of any kind, and certainly did not invent any of the multiplicity of ties which were to bear his name in the course of the century.

The *cravate sentimentale* also carried a warning — it is, Le Blanc insists, only suitable for young men between the ages of 17 and 27, and "after that age it cannot be patronised, by even the most agreeable." In fact, it should be avoided particularly by young men who are not born handsome.

> You, then, whom nature has not gifted with skins of silk — eyes of fire — with complexions rivalling the rose and lily; — you, to whom she has denied pearly teeth and coral lips (a gift which in our opinion would be rather inconvenient) — you, in fact, whose faces do not possess that sympathetic charm, which in a moment, at a glance, spreads confusion o'er the senses, and disorder and trouble in the hearts of all who behold you — be careful how you expose to public gaze a head like a peruquier [wig-maker] we repeat – avoid it.

The other mark of the gentleman, post-Brummell, was the care and attention that only a man of means and leisure could afford to devote to his neckwear — and Le Blanc had plenty of advice about the proper, which is to say, gentlemanly, way to achieve an effect.

"Lesson One — Preliminary and Indispensable Instructions" details an entire strategy for the correct approach to tying the cravat, starting with type of materials chosen for the neckcloth. "The white cravat, with spots or squares, is received as half-dress; but the plain white alone is allowed at balls or soirées," Le

Right: *The Dandies' Coat of Arms* **by George Cruikshank, 1819. The motto is Dandi, Dando, Dandum. The two supporting dandies are monkeys, a common conceit of the satirist. The blazon runs as follows: "A pair of Stays full padded, supporting a Cravat and Collar Rampant."**

3. George Cruikshank: "The Dandies *Coat of Arms*" (1819)

THE DANDY

The extreme cleanliness which Brummell stressed was part of being a gentleman of fashion resulted in horrifying laundry bills for the would-be dandy, as Prince Ludwig of Pueckler-Muskau of Germany discovered when he visited London from 1826 to 1829.

"I send you the following statement by my 'fashionable' washerwoman who is employed by some of the most distinguished 'elegants' and is the only person who can make cravats of the right stiffness," he wrote. The list that followed, which became known as the "Neccessities of a London Dandy," included 20 shirts, 24 pocket handkerchiefs, 30 neck kerchiefs, nine or ten pairs of summer trousers, one dozen waistcoats and stockings a discretion.

"I see your housewifely soul aghast," continued the Prince. "But as a dandy cannot get on without dressing three or four times a day the affair is *tout simple.*"

The four outfits needed each day were a breakfast toilette of chintz dressing gown and Turkish slippers; morning riding dress of frockcoat, boots and spurs; a dress coat and dress shoes for dinner; and ball dress, with dress shoes as thin as paper. Each of these outfits necessitated a different cravat, specially starched and arranged to complement the formality or otherwise of the costume. It was no wonder that washerwomen could be "fashionable" and an important part of every fashionable man's life.

Above: Caricature by George Cruikshank, *c*1830. Dandies drinking tea in morning riding dress, the second of four changes of clothes needed for each day.

Blanc's eager pupil is informed. "The black stock, or cravat, is only suited to military men, not on service, who are dressed in plain clothes. As to coloured Cravats, they are entirely prohibited in evening parties."

Having decided on the color and texture of his neckcloths, a man should then ensure that they are correctly prepared for wear. Examine your cravats when they come back from the laundry, Le Blanc commands, "to ascertain whether they are properly washed, ironed and folded; for the purpose of deciding on the exact style in which each may be worn with the best effect." A small, specially made iron is also necessary, so that the discerning gentleman or his valet may correct any errors in the pressing of his neckcloths. And Le Blanc warns, "If these requisites are not carefully attended to, the Cravat immediately fades, and becomes yellow, whilst on the contrary, if properly prepared, it presents an elegant and *recherchée* appearance."

More warnings follow. "When the knot is once formed (whether good or bad) it should not be changed under any pretence whatsoever." In other words, like Brummell, a new tie means a fresh cravat. When a man has satisfactorily arranged his neckcloth, Le Blanc adds, "the finger must be passed lightly along the top, to smooth and thin it, and cause it to coincide with the shirt collar."

The final lesson, of 17 contained in the book, concerns "Important and necessary Observations," among which is the instruction, "In case of apoplexy, or illness . . . it is requisite to loosen or even remove the Cravat immediately." The cravat, Le Blanc reminds the wearer, should also be loosened before sleeping, study or important business, since "It is universally allowed that the least constraint of the body has a corresponding effect in the mind, and . . . a tight Cravat will cramp the imagination."

He also describes a portable cravat wardrobe for the traveling gentleman — 18 inches (45 cm) long by 6 inches (15 cm) wide by 12 inches (31 cm) deep — and its contents:

> 1. A dozen (at least) of plain white cravats. 2. The same quantity of spotted and striped white cravats. 3. A dozen coloured ditto. 4. Three dozen (at least) shirt collars. 5. Two whalebone stiffeners. 6. Two black silk cravats. 7. The small iron mentioned in the first lesson. 8. As many copies as possible of this important and useful work.

Le Blanc's conclusion — "On the Importance of the Cravat in Society" — threatens social disaster for those who fail to observe his lessons:

> When a man of rank makes his *entrée* . . . the most critical and scrutinising examination will be made of the set of his Cravat. Should this, unfortunately, not be correctly or elegantly put on — no further notice will be taken of him.
>
> But if his Cravat is *savamment* and elegantly formed . . . every one will rise to receive him with most distinguished marks of respect, will cheerfully resign their seats to him, and the delighted eyes of all will be fixed on that part of his person which separates the shoulders from the chin — let him speak downright nonsense, he will be applauded to the skies.

This homily also underlines the final purpose of this wickedly funny little book: to tease and manipulate the socially insecure middle classes who were now attempting to push their way into a social world which had always been closed to them. Whoever Le Blanc was, he was most likely an aristocrat and not, if one notes his jibes at the expense of Americans, a Republican, who found such pretension ridiculous and absurd and was determined to make laughing stocks of the unwary.

Other books followed in the wake of L'Empesé/Della Salda/Le Blanc, all equally keen to make money out of the new democracy of costume, but none so witty or satirical.

The Whole Art of Dress! or, The Road to Elegance and Fashion, authored by "A Cavalry Officer", was one such volume. It was published in 1830 and took a far more serious approach to the subject of neckcloths, which are awarded the whole of the third chapter under the title "Cravatiana."

This work draws heavily — and without any sense of irony — on Le Blanc, but recommends far fewer styles and gives homely instructions on the ironing and arrangement of neckwear, perhaps because it was intended as a genuine guide for aspiring middle-class men of limited means. The giveaway is found on the title page, which boasts that the costume it recommends will be achieved "At the ENORMOUS SAVING OF THIRTY PER CENT!!!"

The book describes only three stock styles and nine styles of cravat, and includes explicit instructions on the folding of the cloth, obviously aimed at the man who could not afford a valet to perform this task on his behalf.

The reappearance of the stock just three years after the ebullient Le Blanc had almost entirely ignored them was due to the revival of Prinny's sartorial ambitions. When he became George IV in 1820, the portly monarch, deciding to invent a popular fashion of his own, came up with a formal stock of black velvet with a black satin bow, which was christened the Royal George.

Opposite: George Prince of Wales by George Cruikshank. Pictured here as a glutton, the Prince of Wales was the inventor of the popular fashion for a formal stock of black velvet with a black satin bow christened the Royal George.

"For the last half-century [stocks] have been worn almost exclusively by the army, navy and marines; until first revived into public notice by his late Majesty, in the year 1822, when they immediately became a universal fashion," says the author of *The Whole Art of Dress!* ("late Majesty" refers to Prinny's death in the year of the publication of this book).

> Though at first viewed with a prejudiced and jealous eye by friends of the old school . . . they at length found their way into the opera and ball-room, and became a portion of full-dress costume. But this has only occurred since his Majesty was pleased to display one at Drury Lane theatre.

Prinny's death signaled the beginning of the end of the craze for sublimely inventive neckcloths. His youth, regency and reign had been full of upheavals, social, economic and military, and the huge variety of styles developed for the simple wrapped, knotted and tied cravat had been symptomatic of an attempt by some to come to terms with a changing world. The almost exclusive use of the cravat gave men a safe, restrictive framework, while the different ways of arranging it gave them a chance to demonstrate individuality and show their status.

In America, male neckwear had followed a different path. The success of the Revolution had given men new confidence in their own taste and ideas, which continued to be dominated by the ideals of comfort and practicality. They even invented the first purely American neckwear — the plantation tie, a wide ribbon tied in a loose bow at the neck of a low and soft-collared shirt.

Landowners in the hot, humid climate of the South still felt the need to differentiate themselves from their staff and slaves, but they had seen how little formal neckwear mattered when it came down to action. Like the bandanna before it, the plantation tie was not fashionable or smart in the European sense, but it was truly modern in the way that it put function above adornment, foreshadowing the time when even great aristocrats would have to go to work and would need clothing which allowed them to move freely and comfortably.

The Dandy revolution, with all the social insecurities it implied, passed by most Americans. The early decades of the 19th century were not an easy time for them, and the fine details of costume were low on the priorities of most men.

SPLIT PERSONALITIES

The Baron l'Empesé, the Conte della Salda and the mysterious H. Le Blanc might all have been the same man behind the pseudonyms, but the author was bright enough to throw in some suitably xenophobic comments for the benefit of his different audiences.

L'Empesé, for instance, relays with some relish a story about a British propaganda campaign after Napoleon had finally been defeated at Waterloo in 1815 and the victorious powers had negotiated the second Peace of Paris.

L'Empesé complains that the British, perhaps fearing that the little Emperor might make a comeback, flooded France with kerchiefs and cravats illustrating in foulard their victories at Trafalgar and Waterloo — "*leurs pretendues victoires*", or "so-called victories," as the author puts it. The French, he snorts, would never have demeaned their great military triumphs by commemorating them on flimsy material — "destined, most of the time, for dirty uses" — the French having more enduring and dignified monuments:

Ce n'est pas à de leger tissus, destinés la plupart du temps à de sale usages, que nous confions le soin de perpetuer notre gloire militaire," he writes contemptuously. "*Des monuments plus durables et plus dignes de nous en sont les nobles et eternels despositaires.*

There was a rage for gambling and speculation, yellow fever had ravaged the seaports and, consequently, commerce, and many of the new citizens doubted the wisdom of separating from England. Under the circumstances, it was hardly surprising that the European fashion for ever higher collars and ever more complex cravats did not catch on.

Some ardent republicans did effect the *Incroyable* style made fashionable in France just after their more fearsome revolution. In addition, a few portraits – such as the 1812 miniature of Benjamin Chew Wilcocks held by the Henry Francis du Pont Winterthur Museum in Delaware — show gentlemen in the characteristic high neckcloths, stiffened with whalebone and giving the wearers unnaturally elongated necks.

But the favorite neckwear of the period was predictable — a loose cravat with a soft, freely tied bow. Another popular style in the 1820s was a version of Le Blanc's *cravat à bal* — a simple, elegant neckcloth crossed diagonally at the front of the throat and pinned in place. A prototype Ascot cravat is also seen in some portraits, with a low wrapped neck and softly folded, slightly puffed ends tucked into the waistcoat. Occasionally collars crept up to jaw level, but they rarely threatened to strangle their wearers, as European versions did. Starch was used, but not to excess.

In short, if Brummell would have been disappointed by the cut of the average American's coat, he would have approved wholeheartedly of his neckwear, which was as neat, sensible and unrestricting as he could have wished in a largely middle-class nation.

Brummell would have said that the Americans knew their place — but he would have been wrong. Confident in their growing strength, excited by the prospects for their young country, hard-working, tough and realistic, most Americans simply did not give a damn about the absurdities of European fashion. Many decades would pass, full-scale industrialization would come and great fortunes would be made before they had the time for such things.

Above: Colonel Sanders shown wearing the popular American Plantation tie.

Affluence and Influence: 1830–1870

Above: A plate from *Le Follet Courrier des Salons* Lady's Magazine, French, *c*1830 showing clothes for indoor wear by men and women. Both are wearing wrapped scarves, hers sailor-style, his tucked into his jacket.

When George IV died in 1830, the Age of Elegance and the dominance of court and aristocratic fashion died with him.

> I try to take him to pieces, and find silk stockings, paddings, stays, a coat with frogs and a fur collar, a star and blue ribbon, a pocket handkerchief prodigiously scented, one of Truefitt's best nutty-brown wigs reeking with oil, a set of teeth and a huge black stock, underwaistcoats, more underwaistcoats, and then nothing,

wrote the novelist William Makepeace Thackeray about the king he stigmatized as "a genlmn" whose "natural companions were dandies and parasites." It was a dismissal, spiritual as well as literal, of the lavishness, fecklessness and exclusivity of the past, and of those who had believed in the supremacy of kings and their hangers-on — and it was an intimation of the coming approach to dress.

Britain and France were increasingly the thing that Napoleon had mocked: nations of shopkeepers. These proverbial tradesmen, comprising a major part of the rapidly expanding middle classes, had spent the time since the Napoleonic wars watching those who thought themselves superior making fools of themselves in their ridiculous cravats and knife-edged collars. More importantly, they had used the years since Waterloo to consolidate and increase both their numbers and their wealth. They now included not only merchants but also professionals and others in a host of occupations who were ready to impose their own ideals on their countries. Electoral reform was imminent in Britain, and from 1832 and the first Reform Act, many of these men had the right to vote. They intended to insure that life became fairer politically, socially, economically — and sartorially.

Where the aristocracy were extravagant — in morals, dress and spending — the middle classes were prudent. They had, for a while, tried to ape their social superiors with the help of such manuals as *The Art of Tying the Cravat*, but because they did not understand the in-jokes of the social set, they had often got it wrong and been found laughable. What is more, they had in common with their American counterparts a need for clothes that were easy to arrange and comfortable to work in: this mass of people earned their living and could not afford the luxury of extreme styles that took valuable time to arrange and then prevented efficient work. Add to this the very natural urge to express their own personalities through dress, while at the same time the bulk of male costume remained somber and dull, and the scene was set for an explosion of neckwear styles.

Charles Dickens, for example, comments in his *Sketches by Boz* (1836–7) on a man wearing "a wisp of black silk round his neck without any stiffener as an apology for a neckerchief." This could well have been an early bow tie — itself a relic of 17th-century cravat strings, the 18th-century solitaire and the bow which was sewn to the front of many stocks.

Another innovation which emerged in the watershed years between Prinny's death and Queen Victoria's accession was the use of a large cravat as a prototype Ascot-style scarf, swathed round the collar and spread out across the chest to conceal the shirt front and held in place with a stick pin.

Mrs Gore sneers at one such scarf in *The Sketchbook of Fashion* of 1833. "A lumpish gentleman having a tablecloth twisted round his thick throat by way of a cravat," she snaps, neatly fusing snobbish social discrimination with stylistic comment. A stout aristocrat such as George IV might well have been "lumpish" and have had a "thick throat," but Mrs. Gore and her kind would never have said so. The words used in this context clearly mean that both man and neckwear were plebeian, ill-bred — that is, middle class.

Of course, the old guard and their styles did not vanish in a puff of smoke the moment their patron, the King, ceased to be. Stocks were still worn by the military, the formally minded and the court, although not with full evening dress. There was even new technological help for those who favored this style – stiffeners patented in 1837 and made of a "frame of oval-shaped springs of steel."

Below left: A plate from the *Petit Courrier des Dames*, 1842, which, despite its French title, was an English publication. The large prototype Ascot cravats are held in place by stick pins. The Royal College of Art, London.

Below: *Going the Whole Hog*, 1853. Hairy Sam is apeing the Count d'Orsay with a fashionably soft, shiny cravat.

Petit Courrier des Dames.

GOING THE WHOLE HOG.

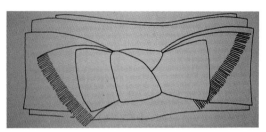

Above: A design for a highly ornamental stock with fringes, *c*1848 made by Alex Grant & Bros., Wood Street, London.

The less extraordinary cravat styles which had been developed over the previous decade also persisted, often with some small modifications which would make them easier to tie and wear, and sometimes appearing under different — often simpler — names. Interestingly, these old-fashioned cravats increasingly became known as "ties," as if creating a new generic term would instantly update them. The *Orientale*, for example, became known as the Eastern tie; the *Américaine* became the Yankee; the *Irlandaise* was transformed into the Hibernian tie; and the Maharatta became the Indian.

Even the use of the word "Dandy" changed, until it meant not a Brummellian figure of extreme neatness and both moral and sartorial probity, but a bit of a show-off with a theatrical passion for clothes. These dandies were far less likely to be contemptuous of the first middle-class neckwear styles than their stodgier contemporaries, and some were quick to adopt them in the hope of setting a trend. "Some exquisites wear a white satin cravat spread out over the breast so as to entirely conceal the shirt," reported *The Gentleman's Magazine* early in the 1830s, noting the adoption of Mrs Gore's reviled "tablecloth."

However, one famous dandy outlived the heyday of his kind, and managed to become almost as famous as the great Brummell himself.

Count d'Orsay represented the finest flowering of the latter-day, butterfly dandy. Like Brummell, he believed that clothes were of paramount importance. Unlike Brummell, his style had no social or moral implications. His appeal was more that of a film or rock star than that of a sartorial reformer — he was an entertainer rather than a crusader and was often greeted on the streets of both Paris and London by cheering crowds.

Count Alfred Guillaume Gabriel d'Orsay was an Anglo-Frenchman from a rich, bourgeois, provincial family who had bought their title in the 18th century. His father, Count Albert, had been one of Napoleon's generals, but after his emperor's escape from Elba, the family had fled to England where their son was introduced into society in 1821, when he was 20 years old.

Like any determined modern celebrity, D'Orsay proceeded to acquire a colorful personal life, leaving England to travel on the Continent for seven years with the wealthy Lord and Lady Blessington. On their return journey, in 1829, Lord Blessington died. He left his substantial fortune to his protégé, on condition that D'Orsay married one of his teenage daughters. Sight unseen, D'Orsay took 15-year-old Lady Harriet Gardiner, Lord Blessington's daughter by a previous marriage, but continued to share his household with her stepmother until, four years after the wedding, the poor girl fled, leaving her middle-aged step-parent and young husband to establish a famous salon at Gore House in Kensington, London — the site on which the Royal Albert Hall now stands.

The unlikely pairing of dandy and matriarch caused considerable gossip and much speculation, even though D'Orsay officially lived in an annex of the house — "a small bijou, for such it is described, adjoining." By the mid-1830s, the couple had become so famous that cartoonists were running caricatures of "BLESS-'N-TON" and D'Orsay was hailed as the leader of high fashion.

He favored soft, curving lines — unlike Brummell's firm, square, shapes or the spiky silliness of the dandies of the previous decade — and sensuous colors and textures. "Inside the open curve of the coat lapels could be seen the curve of the waistcoat lapels," writes Ellen Moers in her book *The Dandy* (1960).

Sometimes D'Orsay wore a white cravat but as often a neckcloth of shiny black satin (Brummell abhorred this style and only wore it when he was too poor to afford clean linen); and the neckcloth was not starched and folded crisply into place by a movement of the chin, but rippled softly and glossily through the open curve of the waistcoat.

Published by James Fraser, 215 Regent Street, London

The look was not conventional, but it was attractive, especially when D'Orsay introduced glossy, soft pastels into his costume through his choice of cravat. Benjamin Haydon took a painterly interest in the effect, praising "such a dress . . . white greatcoat, blue satin cravat, hair oiled and curling." And Jane Welsh Carlyle describes D'Orsay's visiting costume in 1839 with a mixture of horror and fascination:

Right: *Baron Schwiter* by
Delacroix (1798–1863) *c*1826. A
white cravat was often worn to
contrast with black clothes.

At first sight his beauty is of that rather disgusting sort which seems to be, like genius, "of no sex." And this impression is greatly helped by the fantastical finery of his dress; sky-blue satin cravat, yards of gold chain, white French gloves, light-drab great-coat lined with velvet of the same colour, invisible inexpressibles, skin-coloured and fitting like a glove . . . but his manners are manly.

Another of D'Orsay's favorite cravats — which, by this stage, were often tied more like a modern Ascot than a stiff Regency neckcloth — was of primrose yellow satin, and he also wore sea-green quite regularly. All these colors complemented his unusual auburn curls and ruff-like beard.

D'Orsay even felt free to leave his neck uncovered, which, again, drew mixed reports. His friend, Lord Lamington, Talks about D'Orsay's riding clothes in terms of great admiration and approval:

> I have frequently ridden down to Richmond with Count D'Orsay. A striking figure he was in his blue coat with gilt buttons, thrown well back to show the wide expanse of snowy shirt front and buff waistcoat. He was the very *beau-ideal* of a leader of fashion.

Others most emphatically disapproved. "He wears his shirt without a neckcloth, fastened with diamonds and coloured stones," snorted Lady Holland. "In short — a costume that men disapprove as effeminate and non-descript."

However, the softness of D'Orsay's neckwear, its prettiness and elegance were generally much admired, especially among Americans who felt no need to disparage somebody who dressed more beautifully than anybody in their own country. "He is the divinity of dandies," wrote one young man who had seen the count in London. "In another age he would have passed into the court of the gods, and youths would have been sacrificed to the God of fashion."

Instead, in the mid-19th century less puritanical Americans took up D'Orsay's soft styles and copied his less *outré* colors, sea-green in particular enjoying a vogue in both France and America in the 1840s. They also paid him a greater tribute than any he received in Europe, commemorating the Butterfly Dandy he typified with an annual cover of *The New Yorker* magazine devoted to a D'Orsayesque figure — and a butterfly.

His only other lasting memorial was the introduction of the black and white color scheme still deemed correct for most formal evening functions. D'Orsay was so popular that he succeeded in banishing Brummell's elegant blue coat and

Left: The man is wearing the type of neckwear "A Colonel" growls about – a blue bandanna-style cravat with white spots.

Above: A man wearing a modest example of an Osbaldiston. Osbaldistons were usually rather larger and more flamboyant than this.
Below: A group of children, early 20th-century, the two boys wearing sailor suits. The sailor scarf is a variation of the typical Jolly Tar sailor scarf actually worn by sailors.

white cravat in favor of a black coat with a black tie, as worn today. He also had the subtlety to update the black evening stock, the Royal George, and its rigid cravat-style successor, substituting a soft, bowed cravat.

The Gentleman's Magazine of Fashion reported in 1838 that the white cravat

was driven from all decent society by Geo. IV. He discarded the white cravat and black became the universal wear. William IV attempted to revive the white but scarcely succeeded . . . The very courtiers invited to dine at the royal table still wore the black cravat and carried a white one in the hat crown, to be put on immediately before entering the royal presence and removed as soon as they left.

By 1840, fashion magazines were stating simply "for evening wear a black tail coat, a black waistcoat and the simplest possible buttons" were to be worn, while "the black tie is only admitted for evening parties."

Of course, there was not merely one middle class, creating and demanding forms of neckwear. Queen Victoria had begun her long reign in 1837, and under this most middle class of monarchs, the emerging mass of respectable money-earners was not only encouraged to thrive, but to rise. This created a hierarchy within a hierarchy, with an upper middle-class sub-aristocracy of university-educated lawyers, doctors and professionals; a lower middle class of small tradesmen, farmers and superior artisans; and a great swathe in between who ran their own prosperous businesses or worked in a white collar capacity for other people. The neckwear of each man proclaimed his current position in society and, since the great middle class was socially mobile, it also proclaimed his aspirations. As a rough rule, the further a man stood up the social scale, the more conventional and quiet his neckwear would be; the further down he was placed, the brighter and more varied his neckwear became.

So the lower middle-class "Sporting Gent." of the 1848 book *D'Horsay, or The Follies of the Day* wears the essentially working-class bandanna style — "'I'm a slap-up kiddy' was advertised in the blue and white spotted handkerchief twisted

STICK PINS

With the advent of the scarf necktie in the 1830s came the need for an item of jewelry to secure the wrapped folds of material. The stick pin, with an ornamental head and grooved pin that would not slip out of the slithery silk folds of a necktie, was an instant success, and was made in many thousands of designs and materials until the 1920s.

The earliest pins were simple — small cameos, a single pearl, a plain gem such as a ruby or amethyst. But soon men who wanted to display their wealth and originality were designing their own pins in every imaginable style.

Jane Welsh Carlyle reports an encounter with Count d'Orsay in 1845, when he was wearing a black satin cravat and "one breast-pin, a large pear-shaped pearl set into a little cup of diamonds." In *Twice Round the Clock* (1859), there is a list of commonly seen designs: "The horse-shoe, fox-head, pewter-pot and crossed-pipes, willow-pattern, and knife-and-fork pins." By 1870, *The Tailor and Cutter* magazine was commenting on a "breastpin whose head is formed of the wearer's initials, replacing the horseshoe breastpin." Other unusual designs included wishbones, shells, coins, birds, bugs, tortoises, flies, shields, Maltese crosses, stirrups, kangaroos, bulls' heads, miniature glass paperweights, enameled and jeweled flowers and gold and silver ingots.

When, in 1896, the straight-laced *Tailor and Cutter* declared that a tie pin worn with an Ascot "is the only article of jewellery the correct dresser may wear," the passion for pins grew even greater, and the pins — the sole admissible item of adornment for the cultured man — grew increasingly extravagant.

Etiquette writers such as the "Major," the author of *Clothes and the Man* (1900), were quick to warn of vulgarity. "I don't recommend any man to get a diamond pin, or one of pearls or coloured stones surrounded by diamonds," warns the writer. "A diamond pin is not necessary to any man." Instead, he suggests, "nothing beats a plain single pearl" — never a fake — although he does concede that newly fashionable turquoise pins which had become popular in the United States could look good on light-colored ties.

With the establishment of the modern four-in-hand tie as standard neckwear in the wake of World War I, stick pins were replaced by tie pins and clips. Now they are only seen with a formal Ascot cravat at weddings and European royal race meetings, when they are almost invariably single plain pearls.

round his neck," reports the author. And the anonymous author — "A Colonel" — of *the Habits of Good Society* (1855) growls, "Unless you are a prize fighter . . . why should you patronise a neck-tie of Waterloo blue with white spots on it, commonly known as the 'bird's eye' pattern, and much affected by candidates for the champion's belt."

The Joinville (or De Joinville) style — aristocratic, glamorously European — appealed both to romantic upper middles and aspiring lower middles, and won wide popularity. It was a knotted necktie — named after one worn by the Prince de Joinville when he visited Queen Victoria at Windsor in 1843 — with short, squared-off fringed ends, which gave an effect not unlike a long bow tie. Its fame spread so far that a later American tie which bore no resemblance to the original was also named a De Joinville toward the end of the 19th century.

The Byron tie – the second to be given the poet's name during the century — was attractive to men with artistic and individualistic pretentions, being worn by the young of all the middle classes. Unlike its Regency predecessor, which was a large floppy bow, this Byron was a shoestring tie of the kind later to be worn in Hollywood movies by Mississippi riverboat gamblers or tough-minded sheriffs moving in to clean up some beleaguered town. Surprisingly, the satirical magazine *Punch* — which traditionally disapproved of any unusual fashion — applauded it. "An elegant substitute for the cravat is a bit of *mousselaine de laine* a few inches long or a broad bit of shoe string to which the *recherché* name 'Byron tie' has been given," it noted in 1843.

Right: Charles Dickens (1812–70) aged 47 by William Powell Frith RA (1819–1909) in fine clothes. Victoria and Albert Museum, London.

Stocks still lingered, usually worn without the bow in front, and there was a mode, normally within the upper and central swathes of the middle classes, for a necktie called the Osbaldiston (also spelled Osbaldaston). This was a soft cravat tied with a bulky, barrel-shaped horizontal knot from which the short ends dropped onto the outer edges of the gap between shirt and waistcoat — a stylistic compromise between the old, intricately knotted cravats of the Regency and the D'Orsay-influenced softness of the new queen's reign.

But most conventional and upper middle-class men had taken the draped, knotted or pinned neck scarf as their uniform. This was one of the two most popular and enduring styles of the era — the other being the soft, flat bow tie — and was in general use until the First World War. It was eventually adopted at every level of middle- and upper-class society, in every imaginable color and material, and was sold readymade around the world. Its great advantage — apart from its ease of arrangement and the choice of material it allowed — was that, while it allowed a staid, upper-class man to look rich, somber and dignified, it also gave younger men with louder, less refined or lower-class tastes a chance to use bright colors and unusual textures.

Since it needed to be held in place with a stick pin, it also gave men the rare opportunity to flaunt personal jewelry — and hence wealth. Etiquette writers warned sternly against too vulgar a pin, but the newly rich, the young and ebullient did not care. This form of neckwear and its accessories were fun; unless they were openly snubbed for their cheap taste, they wore what they pleased.

Charles Dickens typified this new breed of men – gents, rather than gentlemen — who brought to the fore energy, intelligence and the sort of taste which made the etiquette authorities blanch.

He had been born the son of a government clerk in 1812, but spent an ill-educated and impoverished childhood after his father was imprisoned for debt. By the early 1830s, he had become a newspaper reporter, covering debates in Parliament, until, in April 1836, the serialization of his first novel, *The Pickwick Papers*, made him a literary lion and brought him wealth and fame. Young Dickens was delighted, and proceeded to indulge in all his wildest sartorial fantasies — flamboyant waistcoats, embroidered neckties and loud jewelry among them.

His style sprang from the prevailing fashions among would-be young men-about-town of the lower middle classes, the sort of Jack-the-lads who held down jobs as clerks and gathered on street corners to compare the finery they had acquired from the new Gents. Outfitters where they bought readymade trousers in gaudy checks, huge bright blue-and-white spotted neckerchiefs, and extraordinary stick pins made of electro-gold which, according to *Punch*, looked like "large white currants with gilt eels twisting around them" or "blanket pins with water on the brain."

So when he had the money to indulge himself, Dickens proceeded to splash out on better versions of much the same fashions. He wore such oddities as Cossack trousers, a voluminous garment gathered at the ankle, set off by scarf neckcloths

Left: *Portrait of A Woman* by an anonymous photographer, *c*1855. The young lady is wearing no less than four types of neckwear – a lace collar, a choker held in place with a butterfly brooch and underneath, a stylized man's sharp-ended bow tie. A necklace appears to hang from the tie.

Right: Isambard Kingdom Brunel by Robert Howlett, 1857. The most famous portrait of Brunel shows him wearing a bow tie and is still widely reproduced today. This picture was said to be used by Brunel himself as his *carte de visite*.

in scarlets, greens, purples and stripes. For evening, he concocted a costume which featured a puffed-out shirt frill and a white cravat ornamented with a bow "about eight inches wide!" as one astonished observer wrote in his diary.

By the time that Dickens embarked on his first tour of America in 1842, his outfits were enough to shock the stuffy Bostonians who flocked to his lectures. His waistcoats, in crimson and brilliant green velvet, caused the most tutt-tutting, and although he had brought along one black satin evening waistcoat, it was heavily embroidered with flowers and worn with a black neckcloth traced with colored embroidery and secured with two large diamond pins.

"Mr. Dickens' vivid taints were very conspicuous," protested a young lady in Boston. Another, who saw him in Cincinnati later in his tour, confessed to "considerable disappointment," complaining that he was "easy, negligent, but not elegant." Charles Henry Dana went further. "You cannot get over the impression he is a low bred man," he wrote. "He has what I suppose to be the true Cockney cut."

Dana was not alone in being rather disapproving of the rising man. Peter Buchan had written in *The Eglinton Tournament and Gentlemen Unmasked* (1840):

> The title of Gentleman is now commonly given to all those that distinguish themselves from the common sort of people . . . Indeed, almost at all times, among the vulgar a suit of fine clothes never fails of having the desired effect of bestowing on its wearer the name of Gentleman, without any other qualification whatsoever . . . To the tailor and barber alone, hundreds are indebted for the title of Gentleman.

As the century approached its halfway mark, more and more men with the same sort of background as Dickens rose to prominence in trade, art and literature. The old definitions of a gentleman — a creature born, not made, in whom blue blood and aristocratic manners were the most important components — had to be redrawn and were replaced by Cardinal Newman's moral concept of "one who never inflicts pain . . . is never mean in his disputes."

It was an egalitarian ideal, one to which any man could aspire. Its appropriateness for the times was emphasized by the revolutionary explosions that took place across Europe in 1848, with uprisings in Italy, France, Austria and Germany sweeping away old pretensions, establishing new orders and, in several cases, unifying nations.

Everywhere the young and the middle class were pushing for more informality, more excitement, a bigger share of the action. For women, this meant being more open, more positive, and more natural than ever before, and by 1857,

---

PHOTOGRAPHIC VISITING CARDS

The advent of the photographic visiting card — a process patented by French photographer André Adolphe Disderi in 1854 — meant that the lower middle and working classes could afford to own good and durable likenesses of themselves.

Portraits had before always been the prerogative of the rich, because having one painted could cost hundreds of pounds, but in England, a good photographer charged no more than a guinea (one pound, one shilling) for a dozen of these small images, and a cheap operator might present a bill for a mere few shillings.

The craze for photographic visiting cards was not, however, limited to the lower classes. Cartomania soon swept the world, and even Queen Victoria collected albums full of pictures of friends and of the famous, many of the latter

having sold at a shilling apiece. An 1867 portrait of Alexandra, Princess of Wales, and her baby Louise sold more than 300,000 copies, and by 1869, between three and four million copies of celebrity *cartes de visite* were produced in England alone.

Since these pictures — of the famous and unknown alike — were often close-up head-and-shoulders portraits, the choice of neckwear was unusually important as this would be one of the main features of the finished print. The many surviving cards detail the best and most flamboyant ties of the time, from wrapped scarves and early four-in-hands to ribbon and bow ties, from women's feminine arrangements of bows and brooches to the high, stock-style neckwear favored by some adherents of the Rational Dress Movement.

WALTER MUDFORD, PHOTO, TIVERTON.

WALTER MUDFORD PHOTO. TIVERTON

MAULL & POLYBLANK. LONDON.

It is now thought clever for young ladies to be loud, positive and rapid; to come into a room like a whirlwind; to express ideas of their own in language which, twenty years ago, would only have been understood in the stable.

This change in approach began, of course, to be reflected in female clothes. Riding was a passion among young women of quality, and for this — as for later sporting fads — they adopted masculine-influenced dress: tailored riding habits and stock or bow tie neckwear.

But the greatest influence on women's costume of the 1850s was an American woman called Amelia Jenks Bloomer, who believed that women should abandon their huge skirts, cage crinolines and heavy corsetry in favor of more rational clothing which would allow them to move freely, easily and naturally. Her special contribution was a pair of frilly trousers, named "bloomers" in her honor. Although almost everybody laughed at her early attempts to free women from clothes that quite literally shackled them, within 20 years the Rational Dress Movement that she inspired was in full swing and by the end of the century her principles were seen as the norm, not wild freaks of fancy.

However, in 1851 when she visited England, only a few of the more adventurous dared to put her ideas into practice. *Handley Cross* describes

THE BLOOMER POLKA

Above: An engraving of Mrs Amelia Bloomer by J. J. Blockley, *c*1851, shows her wearing exaggerated bloomers and a length of matching yellow material hung around her neck.

> her lovely daughter Constantia in the full-blown costume of a Bloomer . . . in her silver-buttoned vest, with a flowing jacket above a lavender-coloured tunic and white trousers, fingering her cambric collarette and crimson silk necktie above her richly figured shirt with mock diamond buttons scattered freely down the front.

Despite this flattering report, the magazine advised ladies to have nothing to do with these inelegant garments, of which only the tie was to become immediately common, and then only as part of sporting costume.

For men, the change in atmosphere meant feeling less constricted by rigid etiquette and equally rigid clothes. The lounge jacket — ancestor of the modern business suit — became a favorite for morning wear, for the country, for any occasion when lounging around was possible. If trousers and waistcoat were made of the same material to produce what we would call a suit, the ensemble was named a "Ditto."

This new jacket, loose, comfortable and exposing a larger amount of shirt front than had previously been normal, demanded new neckwear. There were broad bow ties, sometimes known as cravats. There were soft, large Joinvilles, two examples of which were described in *Mr. Sponge's Sporting Tour* in 1853 as "A most extensive once-round Joinville" and "a wide-stretching lace-tipped black Joinville." There were bootlace ties, "not half so broad as a watch ribbon," according to *Punch*, which suggested, "You will be wearing your shoe-string for a neck-tie next." And, of course, there were increasingly more wrapped, knotted and pinned scarf styles.

The raging pace of industrialization, the repeal of the Corn Laws and a new emphasis on free trade and market forces — all linked to technological advances — meant the availability of a greater choice of materials in a wider range of colors, and mid-Victorian men were keen to try them.

"Collars and ties in all the hard names usually found in this branch of trade," one hosier in Devizes, Wiltshire was advertising in 1858, confident that men would be fashion conscious enough to be familiar with a wide range of styles. Some were very adventurous. Mr. Verdant Green, in 1853, made an increasingly common choice when he visited his tailor: "one of the unpretending mop-like coats and vest and trouserings of a neat, quiet, plaid pattern in red and green

Opposite: A fairly typical group of mid 19th-century merchant class men, probably draftsmen, *c*1857. The two men on the left in the top row are wearing bow ties (largely obscured by their beards) while the third wears a simple silk cravat with a stick pin. The seated man on the left sports a Belcher and the other a large bow tie.

which, he was informed, were all the rage, together with a necktie of Oxford blue . . . "

By the 1860s, men's clothing was becoming distinctly modern in appearance and the most important influence was sport. Cricket, rowing and walking had become very fashionable, and demanded a far less restrictive costume than the long, tail-coated style suitable for riding. Men had to be able to move freely, and so they turned to the lounge suit. As daywear it might be too relaxed and informal — "one of the very worst styles of dress worn . . . by a limited class of young men," according to *Minister's Gazette of Fashion* — but it was perfect for sport. That settled the major part of the costume: lounge-style outfits in white flannel were soon being made for summer sports, while rustic tweeds were worn for colder-weather pursuits.

But what should go around a man's neck while he was straining at the oars or bowling an over? A wrapped scarf wouldn't stay in place, a bow tie untied itself or ended up lopsided, a shoestring unstrung itself — and a man, even if he were a gent., really could not be seen bare-necked in public.

Nobody knows who did it, but one day a man unwound his scarf and knotted it as if it were the reins of a four-in-hand carriage. This style stayed in place, no matter how active a man might be — and the modern long tie was born.

Of course, it was very different from the ties men wear today. It was not specially designed for the purpose, and must have looked more like a tightly knotted Boy Scout scarf than a modern four-in-hand. It was far shorter than a modern tie; there was no difference in shape between the front and back aprons; and it was softer and more bunched up, although it might have narrowed behind the neck. It may have been a scarf meant to be puffed and pinned high on the chest to fill the gap between neck and waistcoat, but tied four-in-hand, it was comfortable. It allowed a man to move without worrying that his carefully arranged neckwear would unravel, and within a few decades, it would move off the sports field and into the board room and the drawing room.

Men were no longer prepared to suffer the discomfort and bother of straight high collars, and another major change, which was to influence neckties, was the invention of the separate collar, which appeared in four major low-level styles: the dog-collar, the Piccadilly, the Dux and the Shakespeare (also Shakespere and Shakespear).

Each of these looked best with distinct styles of neckwear. The dog-collar — ancestor of the style now worn by some clergy — was a plain stand collar encircling the neck and overlapping in front, which demanded a firmly wrapped and pinned scarf. The Piccadilly was similar, but was the first collar to be detachable from the shirt. The Dux, which led to the wing collar, was a stand-up collar with the tips turned down in front and looked best with bow ties. And the Shakespeare was the forerunner of the modern collar, a turn-down collar which looked good with a four-in-hand or a narrow string tie.

The neckties themselves now needed more resilience and shape than the cravats which had preceded them. Bows (which were still simple strips of material, narrower than scarfs but otherwise mainly unshaped) and scarf ties alike were lined with heavier materials so that they would hold the style into which they had been tied and would also wear out less quickly. They also needed to be shaped for the first time. The simple length of material, which had once been perfectly adequate, would not fit under the back of the new collars, so the backs of neckties were now made narrow and pleated to retain the bulk needed at the front.

By 1865, most men were — as the Devizes hosier of the previous decade had supposed — conversant with a wide range of styles. When costume was drab, different ties gave each individual the chance to express changes of mood and

Left and below left: *Portrait of a Miller* by Erastus Salisbury Field (1805–1900), the man wearing a black stock tie, and the tie itself.

Königl. lithogr. Institut zu Berlin.

attitude and were cheap enough for every middle-class man to be able to afford a selection. The author of *Mr. Facey Romford's Hounds* comments on "The turndown collar and diminutive neck-string of the day," while in Piccadilly, a stylist explains how "I made the smallest of white bows immediately over a pearl stud in my neck" before going out in the evening.

Not every innovation was greeted with as much acclaim as the new collars and the variations in tie fashions. The first mass-market readymade tie was patented in 1864 — "an octagon scarf, the front made of four tabs above the neck pin, with a neckband fastened behind by a hook and eyelets" — and was immediately sneered at by the snobs of the day. For instance, W. S. Gilbert in his *Bab Ballads* (1869) records a pushy lower middle-class man "With a hat all awry/And an octagon tie/And a miniature, miniature glass in his eye."

Made-up ties might not have been socially acceptable in the best circles, but they were big business with the hordes of up-and-coming men who were not quite sure how to arrange their neckwear well. Sweatshops and homeworkers were soon turning out millions of octagons for both the domestic market and for export to the US and Germany, where readymade ties did not carry such a social stigma.

In the United States, confidence and wealth were on the increase and original styles — especially comfortable bows — began to appear in the magazines of the 1850s. These, with names such as "The Man-About-Town", were among the earliest signs that the U.S. was developing a self-confidence in her independent cultural identity. Until then, all fashion ideas — as distinct from practical innovations — had been imported from Europe.

Ribbon and string ties — quick, easy and economical — were popular, while the cravat-based scarf in a wide variety of materials provided a more formal option. Scarfs were made of cotton plaids and striped silks, satin, taffeta, cotton and wool or silk and wool mixes, silk twills and brocades.

The heterogeneous nature of American communities also led to a greater variety of styles and ideas than were to be found in any single part of any European country. The huge influx of Irish immigrants escaping the potato famines of the 1840s, for example, brought with them a liking for jaunty, country-colored styles in greens, browns and gingers, as well as a preference for scarlet bow ties which were the closest to the red knotted neckerchiefs they had worn at home in Ireland.

Opposite: Felix Bartholdy-Mendelssohn wearing a black satin cravat or a soft stock, with a bow, after d'Orsay.

SPORTING COLORS

The oldest set of sporting colors on record belongs to the I Zingari Cricket Club. This was founded by a group of young Cambridge University undergraduates who enjoyed both the game and amateur theatricals and met at the Blenheim Hotel on London's Bond Street from 1845.

One bright spark decided that they should adopt a set of colors which could be printed on a flag and flown from the cricket pavilion while they were playing. They chose black, a carroty bright red and gold, to symbolize "out of darkness, through fire, into light." These colors were later translated into blazers, caps and ties toward the end of the century.

Another very early set of colors belongs to the Free Foresters Cricket Club. Two years after its foundation in 1856, red, green and white were adopted for the members.

The public school Wellington College, which was founded in 1853 and specialized in educating the sons of soldiers, was also quick to adopt its own sets of colors. Its rugby team played in orange-and-black striped jerseys, while its cricket team sported light-blue caps piped with yellow — colors taken, curiously but appropriately, from the ribbon of the Crimean War medal.

In addition, the often impoverished backgrounds of the new settlers moving into virgin territory, where communications were usually poor and luxuries such as neckties had to be kept and worn for a long time, led to technical innovations. American neckties were being lined with heavier materials several decades before the practice became common in Europe. However, in the U.S. durability was the aim, not — as it was across the Atlantic — a wish to hold complex styles more firmly.

Fashion was still low on the priorities of rural communities, and even in the growing cities of the South and East, men were generally more conservative in their taste than the lower middle-class European masses — something which staider visitors found admirable. "In Boston I saw men more elegant and refined than on the streets of London," one young woman visitor from Britain in 1852 confided in her diary.

The formality of their neckties, so manly and so muted in colour, is a great and pleasing change from the vulgarity to be seen in our Capital.

I suppose it may be that they do not believe in flaunting themselves, or that

Above: Two women in smart casual clothes both modeled on male items, the woman on the left in a sailor suit.

SAILOR STYLES

With yachting all the rage, and Britannia ruling the waves, it would have been surprising if nautical fashions — and, in particular, the distinctive draped and knotted scarf neckwear of the sailor — had not caught on. However, although some women did don sailor-style blouses for sportswear and sailing, naval styling had its greatest effect on the design of clothes for small children.

The sailor suit became a classic outfit for young boys from the moment it was launched in the 1860s. "A boy before he rises to the dignity of trousers and jacket is never so happy as in a Middy suit or a Jack tar, and these suits are now selling in thousands," said *The Lady's World* in 1887. By 1905, sailor suits and blouses were in huge demand in the United States, and Sears Roebuck was advertising a boy's blouse suit, the "blouse . . . trimmed with black tape and two rows of silk soutache," for $1.35.

Boys still love the sailor suit today. Variations on the original theme are still extremely popular and are often seen on the little pages at society weddings. Modern girls, too, perpetuate the trend with sailor dresses. On both boys and girls, the distinctive blouse with its wide neck, edged by a sailor scarf, which frames a triangle of white undershirt, is almost unchanged, making the sailor suit the most up-market reminder of the silk and cotton bandannas worn by sailors all over the world in the 18th century.

such persons are too hard at work to be concerned with low fashions, but the effect is very modest and pleasing.

In the next decade everything was to change. The American Civil War meant fashion was the last thing on men's minds between 1861 and 1865 — but, indirectly, it led to the start of mass manufacturing. All the thousands of soldiers needed uniforms, and vast sweatshops were set up in New York and Chicago, in Richmond, Savannah and New Orleans. After the surrender at Appomattox, these manufacturing bases were to be turned to civilian use in the great garment industry boom of the late 19th century.

But the immediate postwar period was one of almost unrelieved drabness and labor. David L. Cohn, in *The Good Old Days: A History of American Morals and Manners as Seen Through the Sears Roebuck Catalogs*, explains: "Probably at no period in the country's history were empire builders and ditch diggers more shabbily and sloppily dressed than during that great era of national growth."

They were to reap the benefits very shortly — and one of the benefits that American men most enjoyed was a huge range of brilliantly colored, excitingly styled neckwear.

Above: *Three Sailors*, artist unknown, *c*1852. The Jolly Tar on the right sports a sailor scarf.

Above: A group of sailors sporting red scarves, worn inside the collar. *c*1855.

The Old School Tie: 1870–1914

Above: A fine example of an Ascot cravat.

Britain was at her most powerful at the end of the 19th century. The sun never set on her empire, great swathes of the world map were colored imperial red, while industry, the economy and national self-confidence were at an all-time high. Everything Britain made, thought and believed was exported around the globe — and the world was eager to absorb everything on offer.

One of the most striking results of this was that, for the first time, almost everybody in Britain could afford to be fashionable and to change their dress styles with far more frequency than had ever been possible in the past — and for men, fashion had come to be symbolized by neckwear.

No other item of clothing could update an outfit as quickly or as cheaply as a necktie — but no other item of clothing held so many social pitfalls for the unwary. Bright colors betrayed lower middle-class origins, as did startling patterns, and readymade ties — but on the other hand, readymade ties were easy to arrange, while bright colors and startling patterns cheered up drab suits. No wonder etiquette manuals proliferated and sportswear became more popular than ever. At least it provided classless clothing, and if a man belonged to a club, he could freely indulge his taste for bright colors in his association's tie, without instantly being branded a cad.

This emphasis on color and cut rather than on any specific style or styles had its roots in the 1870s, when the last innovations in neckwear shapes — apart from novelty styles and those dictated by advances in production techniques — took place. Ever since that decade, men have worn ties based on a limited number of late Victorian styles.

A fad for high-buttoned suits that continued through to the 1880s led to these final innovations. Narrow bow ties, which could be worn without comment today, grew out of old bowed-cravat styles and were popular because they didn't get buried under climbing lapels. The Ascot, too, arrived in this decade, since the gently folded or puffed top of the scarf emerged neatly at the neckline.

This enduring style took its name from the Royal Ascot race meeting which had been taking place in Berkshire since the late 18th century. The name may have been an attempt on the part of a canny manufacturer to convince aspiring gents of the tie's aristocratic connections, or it may have been bequeathed by some inventive race-goer.

Its early form was strictly prescribed. The simple Ascot was made in plain material, initially silk, and was 50 inches (127 cm) long. The back of the neck was ⅞ inch (2.2 cm) wide, to slip under the collar, and the ends were 3 inches (7.6 cm) wide, squared and sewn closed. A variant was the puffed or puff Ascot, named for the puff of material formed in the center of the neck at the front and commonly made in woven foulard in striking colors such as primrose scattered with claret, blue or green. Both types were sold readymade in large numbers.

There was even an ingenious justification for the new high-necked styles. According to *The Gentleman's Magazine of Fashion* in 1875, "Medical men ascribe many deaths during the past winter to the fashion of low collars and to gentlemen not being sufficiently protected by their clothing at the throat and neck."

THE ESTHETE WITH THE GREEN TIE

One of the most enduring images of the late 19th century is the figure of the esthete — perhaps Oscar Wilde — who believed in reform of the male dress as passionately as Amelia Bloomer had espoused the liberation of women from their crinolines and stays. The apostles of the Aesthetic Movement, which thrived between 1878 and 1884, advocated a return to ancient styles: for men, a modification of the garb of a Cavalier courtier; for women, neoclassical drapery.

Wilde in particular summed up *fin de siècle* decadence in his costume as the self-proclaimed "Professor of Aesthetics," with his knee breeches, velvet coat, flowing green tie over wide, turned-down collar and the important accessory of a drooping lily. For the young poet and playwright, this was as much an advertising gimmick as a genuine declaration that men's clothes were uncomfortable — and it was a gimmick that worked, especially in the United States.

Wilde was immortalized in Gilbert and Sullivan's comic opera *Patience* in 1881 and was eventually asked to travel to New York to publicize the opening of the production there. His reply, by cable, to the American entrepreneur in charge of staging the show was typical: "Yes, if offer good." Apparently it was good enough, and he became a nine-day wonder. "Singularity of appearance, wit, rudeness, count doubly in a democracy," Frank Harris wrote wryly, commenting on the lovely Oscar's success.

The outfit, however, did not catch on.

Above: *Oscar Wilde* (1845–1900) by N. Sarony, 1882. Wilde's posture and appearance confirm his studied disdain for contemporary conventional costume and mores.

Above: Aubrey Beardsley (1872–1898) by J-E Blanche (1861–1942). The floppy bow tie worn by Beardsley perfectly matches his suit.

**Above: British costume, 1891.
The man is wearing a reef-
knotted bow tie and the woman
a four-in-hand.**

Presumably highly physically active men were exempt from death due to low neckwear, for the sports boom still swept Britain and comfortable neckwear continued to be worn for a range of activities, which soon took in yachting, skating, cycling and lawn tennis — "this aristocratic and fashionable game" as *The Gentleman's Magazine of Fashion* was to describe it. For all these sports the four-in-hand tie was normal wear — although a sailor's tie, knotted in a kind of reef or square knot with its ends dangling at either side of the upper chest, enjoyed a lesser vogue lasting until the First World War.

Even the simple style of the four-in-hand had now been formulated. According to C. Willett Cunnington and Phillis Cunnington in their authoritative *Handbook of English Costume in the 19th Century*, "when tied the centre knot presented a horizontal border along the top and bottom. The two ends [were] nearly the same width and cut square; and hanging one over the other down the midline." It, too, was no longer any scarf knotted in a particular way. The new four-in-hand cut specified a tie 41 inches (104 cm) long, arranged so that one end was 15 inches (38 cm) long and the other 7 inches (17.8 cm), with both ends 1¾ inches (4.4 cm) wide.

The marketing men of booming British fashion had gone to work on the four-in-hand as well, sometimes dignifying it by calling it the Derby — presumably after that great race — and sometimes the Oxford. Square-ended bow ties were also, occasionally, known as Oxfords.

This naming of a square-ended tie with a sporting background after the old university was not, in fact, an advertising con. In 1880, the rowing club of Oxford University's Exeter College apparently decided to modify their costume and create the first club or school tie by removing the ribbon hat bands from their boaters and tying them, four-in-hand, at their necks. They placed an order for proper ties, identical to their colored hat bands, with a local outfitter on June 25 that year, and the practice spread rapidly.

In the 1880s, the British Army abandoned their traditional gorgeously colored uniforms, which offered far too good a target for enemy sharpshooters. These colors – not just the brilliant red of the battle tunics, but also individual regimental schemes seen in officers' mess jackets, were preserved in their ties.

Some cynics have suggested that these new tie colors were often chosen by the colonel's wife because they looked pretty, but the full dress uniforms of many regiments show the link clearly. Obvious examples include the striped red and green tie of the Royal Rifle Corps, whose uniform had been rifle green with scarlet facings, and the black-and-green striped tie of the Rifle Brigade, whose full dress uniform was green with black facings. The same can be seen in the gray, black and white stripes of the Artists' Rifles and the green and blue stripes of the Inns of Court Regiment.

Soon the public schools joined in, producing school and old boys ties from the 1890s. These schools were enjoying a surge in popularity. An increasing number of them sprang up to give a gentleman's education to the sons of merchants, tradesmen and others whose parents would never have been allowed through their hallowed doors.

Neckwear styles were now fairly static. The string tie popped up again in the 1890s; the scarf covering the shirt front, which rose and fell in the opinion stakes, could, advised magazines, be tied with "one apron making a waterfall." The bow tie was an established favorite, initially as a simple, narrow length of material and then, in the 1880s and 1890s, in recognizable modern shapes — first, the butterfly, with its broad, straight ends, then the batwing, with curved blades.

What was truly new was the search for color, for a tie that meant something, that lent distinction or said, like the new club and school ties, "I belong." New

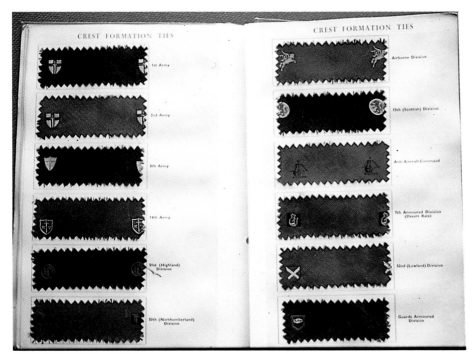

Left: Macclesfield woven silk regimental pattern ties with crests.

colors and patterns in silk were streaming out of the thundering mills of northwest England. The town of Macclesfield led the way in producing innovative designs — with raw materials imported from India and the empire's holdings in China — to satisfy an extraordinarily prosperous and imaginative population.

The search for novelty was tempered by a new snobbishness. By now, the Victorian middle class had grown so vast and male costume had become so much a formula — dark, somber coat or jacket and trousers in a limited number of simple cuts — that the upper echelons were keen to make it clear that they were of superior stock to their similarly clad lower middle-class neighbors. The latter wanted to rise to the middle of the middle class, and the middle middles wanted to become upper middle.

Everybody was straining for social superiority, and neckties were one obvious signpost, especially since the evolution of the club, school and regimental ties. There were hierarchies even in these areas, with the Guards' being a more socially desirable tie than the Rifles', Oxford and Cambridge boat club's ties being more upper-crust than those of the Thames Watermen, Eton's being vastly preferable to that of a new school such as Wellington. However, a public school tie of any type at least told the watching world that the wearer's family had a certain amount of money and that the wearer was pretty much guaranteed to have decent table manners and to speak the Queen's English. Each tie, whether regimental, club, sporting or educational, contained coded information about the wearer's background and aspirations — and the vast Victorian middle class loved them.

In this atmosphere of thrusting snobbishness, there was much they did not love. If an Eton tie opened doors to you, other styles could easily slam them shut, and an entire industry of etiquette and fashion writers was soon busy giving advice to the unwary.

"Few there are who can wear a hunting stock and still look like a gentleman," warned *The Tailor and Cutter* in 1898, although it did concede that this large scarf of cellular cloth, tied twice around the neck without a collar, was perfectly acceptable on the hunting field. The same magazine took an even fiercer stance later that year when discussing neckties in red, crimson or "other sanguinary hues." "How is it that anyone describes a man wearing a red necktie, nothing

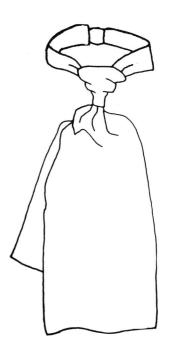

Above: A diagram of a four-in-hand.

Right: 17 patterns for Macclesfield woven silk regimental ties show the variety of colors available in striped designs.

further need be said, you imagine a horsy individual, or a sporting publican with a suit of loud checks, a loud voice, and much jewellery?" they asked nastily.

Other vogues, oddly, found favor, including a brief flirtation with willow-patterned bow ties. These were not, said the magazine, "confined to the orthodox and familiar blue shade in which it [willow pattern] has for such a long time been produced upon our dinner plates . . . it looks particularly smart and dressy in some tones of browns and greens."

When willow-pattern bow ties were applauded and red neckwear of any kind was deemed low caste, it was no wonder that large numbers of men turned to handbooks such as *Clothes and the Man: Hints on the Wearing and Caring of Clothes*, which was written by a pseudonymous "Major" of the newspaper *To-Day* and published in 1900. Any insecure man could follow the Major's very specific advice and be sure that his neckwear would do him credit. For a start, he must choose the right collar. "There is no collar to beat a double collar," this guide states. "A tie that is worn with a double collar simply cannot get out of place; the collar grips it and holds it firmly."

Another piece of advice concerns the best way of adjusting the tie — gently. "Few men make the mistake of drawing their tie up too loosely; most men get savage with their tie when it doesn't go properly, and draw it up very tightly. The result is disastrous." Then there is the question of color. "I have known a man to have on — at one and the same time — a pink shirt, a tie of quite another shade of pink, a scarlet geranium in his buttonhole, and a face the colour of a sunset," says the disapproving Major.

If you are in any doubt as to whether your tie goes well with your shirt, discard it and wear a tie of plain black silk (not satin) or plain white silk. These ties are never out of fashion and they always look well . . . You may wear a dark navy blue tie with a pale blue shirt, but don't put a heliotrope tie with a shirt of the same colour, or a pink tie with a pink shirt.

Finally, the Major relays a dire warning of the consequences of failing to insert a tie pin correctly. A man with a very elaborate pin decorated with sprays of gold wire was, according to the author, visiting the theater one evening with "the lady who had intended to be his wife." The pin worked its way out and began to tickle the poor man's neck until he was finally compelled to scratch it. Unfortunately, he scratched so vigorously that he dislodged a piece of sticking plaster which had been covering a shaving nick, and made his neck bleed. His fiancée promptly fainted "and the engagement is now off," says the stern Major, who adds, "This will show you the folly of wearing your scarf pin in the wrong place."

The right place, apparently, was about 2 inches (5 cm) away from the knot. "It can't work out then. Dig it through the two folds of the tie at once, then out at the front and in again." And woe betide the man who dared ignore these orders.

The worst crime that any Victorian man could commit was to wear a ready-made tie, whether a puff Ascot, a bow or a version of the newfangled four-in-hand christened the Teck, after the Duke of Teck, who was a cousin of Queen Victoria – although this spurious association did nothing to convince the upper and upper middle class man that any kind of readymade tie was acceptable.

Mr. Pooter, in George and Weedon Grossmith's 1892 novel *The Diary of a Nobody*, relates the sorry tale of a trip to the theater in his new bow tie.

I was leaning out of the box, when my tie — a little black bow which fastened on to the stud by means of a new patent — fell into the pit below.

A clumsy man, not noticing it, had his foot on it for ever so long before he discovered it. He then picked it up and eventually flung it under the next seat in disgust . . . To hide the absence of the tie I had to keep my chin down for the rest of the evening, which caused a pain at the back of my neck.

The Major, writing for a less informed audience than those who laughed at Pooter, made his views on made-up neckwear very clear. "Of course, no gentleman ever does wear a made-up tie, and doesn't want the credit (?) of wearing one," he writes firmly. "I consider it the duty of every father to tell his son this on leaving school; it would save him a great deal of heart-burning and anxiety in after life."

In case this did not shock any reader foolish enough to be fond of his readymade neckwear into throwing his whole collection away, he added:

Below left and below: An amazing selection of the enormous variety of styles and types of ties and cravats advertised in Harrods catalogs at the beginning of the 20th century.

BANDANNAS FOR THE WORKERS

The spotted bandanna handkerchief, especially in red and white cotton or silk, continued to be the neckwear of the masses through the 19th century.

London street vendors in particular were greatly attached to their bandannas, which were an established part of their costume. Henry Mayhew, who interviewed many costers and street sellers in 1840, writes, "The man who does not wear his silk handkerchief — his 'Kingsman' as it is called — is known to be in desperate circumstances." (The name "Kingsman" was a relic from the days when such handkerchiefs were contraband: a

"king's man" was a customs officer.)

Mayhew reports that "a yellow flower on a green ground, or a red and blue pattern, is at present in vogue. The women wear their kerchiefs tucked in under their gowns, and the men have theirs wrapped loosely round the neck, with the ends hanging over their waistcoats." Such neckwear is beautifully illustrated in the *Cries of London* series of prints which were popular throughout the century.

The fashion was not exclusively urban. Agricultural workers of both sexes wore

Right: A magnificent portrait of a farmer. He is wearing a scarf knotted around his neck and to his braces to keep the ends out of the way.

Below right: *The Draughts Players* **by G.C. Bingham, 1850. The three styles of neckwear visible are the short bow, the floppy bow and the scarf.**

Below: A fine Indian cotton red bandanna.

bandannas at the throat, and a traveler of the time noted an encounter with "three or four tidy lads with silk handkerchiefs round their necks." Less kindly, a visitor to Leicester races remarked on "the clod-pated yeoman's son . . . his lank hair and silk handkerchief, new for Race time about his neck."

By the end of the century, cheap mass-produced clothes had reached even the working classes, and such old-fashioned, picturesque costumes as agricultural workers' traditional smocks were being replaced by rough modern suits in tough materials such as corduroy. For the very poor, these clothes might come from the great secondhand warehouses which were found in all large cities, but neckties were always bought new.

The bandanna persisted wherever heavy work was undertaken — it was still as comfortable as ever, and it was, even in the late 19th century, a valid form of neckwear. But, increasingly, working-class men bought cheap, readymade neckties for their Sunday best, favoring bows and wrapped scarfs which harked back to the kerchiefs they had worn for so many decades.

Above: A worker wearing a red spotted neckerchief. Mid 19th century.

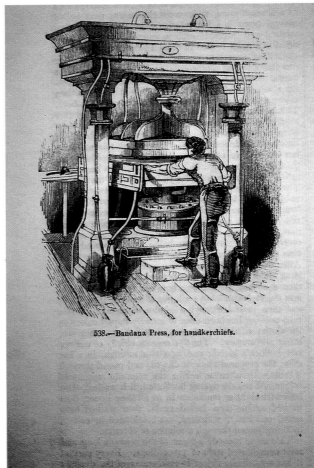

538.—Bandana Press, for handkerchiefs.

Above: A 19th-century bandanna press for printing handkerchiefs.

**Above: The Prince of Wales
*c*1900. He is wearing a four-in-
hand with informal country
wear.**

The young man who tries to get a tie of the same colour as her dress doesn't make such a fool of himself as the young man who goes to a shop and lays in a supply of ready-made ties. He begins to buy them because he thinks they are cheaper than the others; they aren't really any cheaper, because a ready-made tie wears always in precisely the same place, and therefore soon wears out.

So many writers warned the socially sensitive of the perils of readymade neckwear that, by 1906, when the liberal *Daily News* organized an exhibition about industries which took advantage of sweated labor — impoverished workers who often ran their own small workshops or worked from home for a fraction of the wages paid to factory hands — the manufacture of made-up ties was already on the decline.

Snobbery was not the only thing to harm this once-thriving industry, according to writer Ethel Beaumont, who contributed a monograph on tie-making to the exhibition's program. "Englishmen are ceasing to wear made-up ties, and . . . Germans and Americans, who do wear them, and to whom ten or twelve years ago bales of made-up ties used to be shipped from this country, now make their own," she explains.

One of the major problems facing workers in this field was the erratic nature of the tie-buying population. "The times and seasons when men will order new ties are fixed by no law (as even the laws of fashion hardly touch the wearer of made-up ties)," writes Ethel Beaumont.

Consequently, a worker can have no idea as to when she will be slack, nor for how long that dreaded time will last.

Alternating with this come times of great pressure, when the factories have large orders placed with them to be executed quickly . . . a woman will frequently work from 7am till 11pm to complete the order, well knowing that if she did not do so in the specified time, she would run a grave risk of not obtaining another.

Wages were low, with women receiving around 1.25 old British pennies for fabricating a dozen knots, 1.75 pennies for a dozen neckbands and 2 pennies for a dozen fronts. An average weekly wage was seven shillings, which the workers felt was poor: "One worker expressed the feeling that 'it did seem a bit hard to make poplin ties for a halfpenny apiece, when you cannot buy one anywhere for less than a shilling [twelve old pennies].'"

Even in a shrinking market, the demand for readymade ties remained considerable. In its 1902 catalog, Harrods listed made-up knot and pin scarfs for between one shilling to two shillings and sixpence, made-up bows from one shilling to one shilling and sixpence and waiter's "No Band" ties — a clip-on permutation of the made-up bow, which tucked under the stiff collars of the day — for three shillings and sixpence a dozen.

By 1911, when the great store was boasting "HARRODS FOR EVERYTHING — THE SUPPLY CENTRE FOR THE EMPIRE" made-up bows and pin scarfs were still on offer. Meanwhile the social stigma attached to the readymade market was being tackled with a new style of open-ended four-in-hand tie which was tied permanently by the wearer in a slip-knot and then pulled on and off over the head.

Despite the apparently rigid rules governing neckwear, a gradual relaxation took place in the wake of the old Queen's death in 1901. The brief fashion for very high collars and high, wrapped scarfs was abandoned in favor of lower, softer collars, while Victoria's son and heir, Edward VII, did much to promote the acceptability of the lounge suit — with its low V-neckline and accompanying four-in-hand tie — in formal situations. And in 1902 the Vicar of Marlow on the

THE HOUSE OF JAEGER

The late 19th century was a great time for clothing reformers, and one whose name has since become a fashion legend was Dr. Gustav Jaeger of Stuttgart in Germany, who believed that men should dress in undyed wool from head to foot.

His outfit — a gingery tweed knickerbocker suit, teamed with a creamy white woolen shirt, wool collar and wrapped woolly cravat or four-in-hand — was, he believed, very good for the health, encouraging the skin to breathe and stimulating a good blood supply. He was particularly keen on the merits of the woolen collar and cravat which, he claimed, would guard against chest complaints and were good for singers who wished to protect their voices.

Dr. Jaeger's views were taken surprisingly seriously in educated circles across Germany, Scandinavia, Britain and the United States, and he even acquired a famous follower in the writer George Bernard Shaw, who astonished people by wearing his Jaeger outfit in the center of London, among the conventionally dark-suited crowd.

The original Dr. Jaeger's Sanitary Woollen Company, which the great eccentric founded in 1884, is now the Jaeger chain of fashion shops, world famous for selling beautifully tailored, typically English clothes to men and women around the world. They no longer make undyed wool collars and cravats, preferring to sell more predictable Italian silk ties.

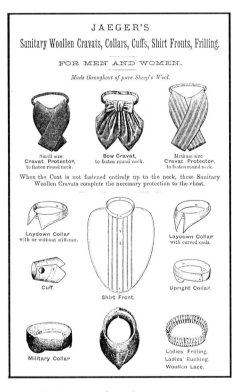

Above: A Dr Jaeger advertisement.

Above: George Bernard Shaw, with Lady Astor, *c*1930 in a Jaeger outfit.

Above: **La Cycliste by Bonvalet. The young woman is wearing a tucked-under bow tie.**

Below: ***The Customs*** by **Mancini, 1837. The young lady is obviously a follower of fashion, wearing a lacy jabot, much favored by the trend-setting women of the day.**

Thames appealed to his potential congregation: "Please do not permit the matter of dress to keep you away [from church]: come in your flannels and boating dress."

More ephemeral styles also had their moments of glory. Khaki ties were a patriotic gimmick after the Boer War at the turn of the century, and *The Tailor and Cutter* predicted a major fashion trend. "Khaki neckties will be much in demand out of compliment to 'The Absent-Minded Beggar,'" they wrote, referring to the huge numbers of men who were unemployed in the aftermath of the conflict. Public mourning after Queen Victoria's death also stimulated demand for black-edged evening bow ties. "On account of the mourning into which . . . people have been plunged, the manufacturers are producing the white cambric bow with a narrow black edge and black embroidery in the corners," reported *The Tailor and Cutter*.

However, in general, the days of neckwear innovation were over. Neckties were now what they are today — a symbol of class distinction, of professional status and a sign of aspirations.

For women, though, the picture was different. Since the 1870s, Amelia Bloomer's principles of rational dress had continued to grip the female imagination, and if most women were not keen to be seen in long frilly knickers, they were determined to adopt a less restrictive form of dress than the overpowering crinolines they had favored in the earlier part of Victoria's reign. The tailor-made costume was exactly what the mass of women were looking for — a man-tailored jacket and free-flowing skirt, worn with a shirt and tie for any active occupation or sport.

The Saturday Review, along with many other journals of the time, disapproved of any outfit which did not have as its primary function the attraction of the opposite sex, insisting, "It is woman's business to charm and attract and to be kept from anything that may spoil the bloom of her character and taste." Women themselves disagreed. They wanted to play tennis, to ride bicycles and horses, to take up archery, to skate, swim and sail — to join their brothers in having fun. If doing all that meant wearing a variation of men's clothes, then they'd cheerfully wear them, especially since, in the melting pot of late Victorian society, the wish to attract the "right" sort of man was balanced by the fear of attracting the "wrong" kind.

And they were not as lacking in femininity as some men believed. They might wear ties, but these could well be pretty bowed ribbons, perhaps lace-edged silk or satin bows, elegantly draped scarfs, tasseled cords or even, in the 1880s, fabulous lacy jabots which harked back to the court of Charles II.

Three years after the Rational Dress Movement was founded in 1881, they held an exhibition where women were seen in long culotte skirts or flowing trousers — paired, of course, with neckties. These, warned the author of *The Science of Dress* (1885), should not be too high.

Tight collars and cravats round the neck cause headaches, by interfering with the circulation, and when the veins of the neck are swollen, as during drunkenness, by their preventing the return of blood from the head, a sort of apoplexy may result and death follow.

This horrid prospect did not deter most women. Even those who did not favor reform took up some of the neckwear, simply because it was pretty and sat well on the high-necked shirts fashionable at the time — "chins are worn very high, just at present," as Oscar Wilde reported in *The Importance of Being Earnest* in 1895.

Cycling in London's Battersea Park and New York's Central Park was all the rage, and brave women even took to wearing knickerbocker suits, "so full that they lack all indecorous suggestion, pleated round the waist and gathered into a band below the knee; long gaiters, Norfolk bodice ending at the waist with a belt, revealing a shirt and tie at the neck." It was as if the presence of a tie turned a potentially immodest woman into an honorary man, who was therefore safe from any imputation that she was not behaving with propriety.

By 1898, *The London Tailor* was hailing — with good reason — the tailor-made costume and its accessories as the only real clothing breakthrough of the era, "which is doubtless due to the active life led now by women of every class."

In the United States, new forms of neckwear were thriving and the former colony came up with one fashion hit that even made its way back across the Atlantic, along with the increasing numbers of wealthy passengers of the great liners.

The Joinville scarf of the 1890s and early 1900s bore no resemblance to the British Joinville of 50 years earlier, being a large scarf looped through a scarf ring rather than a fringed and knotted short cravat. In 1897 the Sears Roebuck catalog boasted of its vast stocks of

> the famous de Joinville scarf, 6in wide, 38in long. The most popular and swellest gentlemen's scarf. Without exception they are the handsomest line of silks ever brought into this country. Over 300 different designs — light and modern colorings. 50 cents, 3 for $1.40.

Strangely, although neckwear in general had been known as neckties since the 1840s in Europe, Americans clung to the word "scarf" as a new generic, referring even to the four-in-hand in this way.

"The Cheapest Supply House on Earth" warned, "An untied man is an untidy man," and also offered such goodies as the 43 cent four-in-hand — "We will be glad to have you compare one of these ties with any 75 cent tie you have ever seen" — and a 50 cent tie, described as "Our price poultice for tired pocket books."

Above: A lower middle-class woman wearing a floppy rough-ended bow tie and a double horseshoe brooch joining the top of her blouse.

Left: The Chelmsford Ladies Cycling Club, 1890. The group is wearing a wonderful mix of four-in-hands, bow ties and cravats. The two men are sporting rather less interesting four-in-hands.

Right: *Man with the Cat* by C. Beaux, 1898. The man is wearing a lovely four-in-hand. USA National Collection.

By 1902, a positive mania for made-up ties had taken hold of the bulk of American men, and triumphant Yankee manufacturers had set up their own industry to compete with readymades coming from Britain. The Americans obviously did not care about the snobbish posturing of their European cousins; made-up ties suited their lives, and they bought them in their millions.

Sears Roebuck offered a dozen versions of the Teck, including catalog no. 34R412: "Our new style Teck scarfs, made to hook in the back. Small knot with wide aprons. A stylish, strictly high grade scarf in large assortment of new silks." This gem cost 45 cents.

Bow ties were also widely popular, especially the shield bow — which had two projections of stiff material such as celluloid to clip neatly behind stiff collars — and the band bow, pre-tied in front on an adjustable neckband fastened with hooks. Children's versions of made-up bows and four-in-hands were also available, usually on an elasticated band. The other thriving and well-established

Left and right: Two images from a Sears Roebuck catalog, 1902.

style was the string tie, which Americans regarded as a permanent part of fashion and not as the novelty it was to Europeans.

Nearly 40 years later, David L. Cohn looked back on this period as the most exciting time yet in American neckwear. Ties manufactured in the early 1900s "had none of the morbid fear of color that marks the efforts of their brethren today," he wrote sadly.

However, the most innovative neckwear — the neckwear instantly evocative of a particular place, time and lifestyle — had evolved in the great new West, where cowboys and bandits alike had taken cotton bandannas, folded them in half and tied them at the back, so that they could be used as dust masks, or simply as masks.

These handkerchiefs were no longer silk but practical, hard-wearing cotton from the South, made and dyed at home on the Eastern seaboard. Courtesy of the aspiring prospectors and would-be cattle barons of the late 19th century, these once working-class kerchiefs became part of one of the most romantic uniforms ever invented. In a typically American inversion, Hollywood was to make them famous in Westerns, and youngsters all around the world would readopt them as a symbol of healthy, virile and independent masculinity.

A World in Conflict:
1914–1945

The rigid etiquette which had governed men's clothing around the civilized world for more than a century died in the trenches of the First World War along with the young British officers who had been brought up to carry on its traditions into the 20th century. Their era of privileged elegance had already been mortally wounded by the onslaught of radio, films, suffragettes, the motor car and airplane. The Great War merely delivered the death blow.

Between 1914 and 1918, great barriers of prejudice crumbled as troops mixed with officers and officers learned to respect their men, as women took to trousers and worked in the munitions factories performing what had always been considered men's jobs, as generations of European economic and social power were ground into the mud of Flanders.

In Britain, shortages made impossible the elegance and choice that well-dressed men had always taken for granted. Pacifists adopted soft shirts and loose four-in-hand ties, while soldiers grew used to more comfortable styles and were reluctant to return to the rigid constrictions of collars and the elaborate arrangements of material of their fathers.

As late as 1917, a doctor, Walter G. Walford, was able to publish a book called *Dangers in Neckwear*. This theorized that a high proportion of the ills besetting mankind — from headaches, dizziness, eczema, sunstrokes and deafness to angina, rheumatism, strokes, apoplexy, tetanus and sudden death — were caused by tight collars and neckties. Within two years, his warnings would have been needless, for by then the tight collar and strangling tie had become part of the past.

The leader in this trend, as in almost every menswear trend of the next 20 years, was Edward, Prince of Wales, later King Edward VIII and later still the Duke of Windsor. He had served as an army staff officer throughout the war, he was young, handsome, charming and forward-thinking, and he rapidly became the idol of millions, adored by women and admired by men.

The Prince liked soft collars and four-in-hand ties — men around the world wore them. The Prince found the lounge suit quite formal enough for daywear — so did other men, everywhere. The Prince preferred dinner jackets to white tie and tailcoats for most of his forays into the newly fashionable night clubs — others instantly followed his lead. "As worn by the Prince" became the catchphrase of every London tailor, while *Men's Wear* in New York reported a

little tartly, "The average young man in America is more interested in the clothes of the Prince of Wales than in the clothes of any individual on earth."

One American commentator summed up his appeal in the most flattering terms:

> His fair and clean-cut good looks were sufficient to make him an idol, considering his position, but he possessed just that combination of conventional good taste and slight but never exaggerated whimsy to make him a fashion idol.

Of course, informality in the aftermath of the First World War was not the same as informality now. The Prince might confess, "All my life, hitherto, I had been fretting against the constrictions of dress which reflected my family's world of rigid social convention. It was my impulse, whenever I found myself alone, to remove my coat, rip off my tie, loosen my collar and roll up my sleeves," but he would never have done such a thing in public. Nor would any but the most extreme of eccentrics or academics. Men continued to wear collars and ties in ever-increasing numbers, as mass production brought more clothes within the grasp of more and more men.

Retired tie-man Myron Ackerman, whose New York firm supplied linings for neckwear, remembers,

Above: A boxed set of gentlemen's fashion accessories including a tie clip and cufflinks made by Gallery of St. James's, London.

Above right: Two highly traditional striped tie designs.

During the First World War, a mass tie craze swept America. Everybody from lather workers to guys on construction sites was wearing a tie — but they were pretty simple ties. The design was non-existent in most cases, the ties were just straight cut strips of fabric about two inches wide.

This inherent conservatism was underlined by some of the consequences of the war. In Britain, it was a matter of pride to be able to wear one of the regimental striped ties, and more men than ever had earned that privilege. Americans, too, had been influenced by what they had seen on the battlefields of France and Belgium and had brought the idea of the striped tie as the mark of an officer and a gentleman back to their own country. At the end of its travels, however, it had changed. Where the stripes on the British tie run diagonally from high on the left to low on the right, the American imitations were — and are to this day — high on the right and low on the left.

Robert Gieves of Savile Row tailors Gieves & Hawkes, who hold Royal Warrants from both Prince Charles, the current Prince of Wales, and from Prince Philip, Duke of Edinburgh, explains that there are two major theories which account for this. "The nicest story is that an American gentleman brought a tie home with him from England and was so pleased with it that he called up his tailor to ask him to make some more," says Mr. Gieve, whose family has been supplying naval uniforms and superlative clothes to discerning men since Napoleon's day. "He stood in front of the mirror and described the tie exactly — only he forgot that he was describing its mirror image, and the result was the high-right, low-left American striped tie."

This story, Mr. Gieve concedes, is probably apocryphal. He believes that the real reason for the mirror-image American striped tie is more prosaic. "European tie makers cut the material with the surface uppermost, while Americans cut on the back," he says. "It's probably as simple as that."

T. M. Lewin & Sons, the British specialists in regimental, club and school ties, offer an even simpler solution to the mystery. "Although most British regimental stripes are high-left, low-right, a few are high-right, low-left," says their Paul Symons. "It may well be that the first tie used as a pattern by an American tie manufacturer was one of these."

The diagonally striped tie came to be seen as a symbol of professional respectability, and every club and society clamored to have a design of its own. For men feeling uncertain in rapidly changing times, one of these striped ties gave the wearer a sense of belonging, of knowing that somewhere there were people who shared his views. Ultimately, the style was copied wholesale by the mass manufacturers, and even a man who didn't belong to a single association could buy a little piece of security at his local outfitters for a few shillings.

The other kind of tie that became fashionable among well-dressed British men was what Americans now call a Macclesfield — a silk tie with a small, regularly repeating design of circles, squares, rectangles ovals, or triangles, which was manufactured in the town of Macclesfield in Lancashire in northwest England. These ties were to become the biggest fashion hit of the 1920s with American men who could afford the best styles.

However, all these ties had an inherent problem. They were, essentially, simple strips of material cut along the grain of the fabric and lined with a heavier material to give them some resilience. Because they were subjected to daily knotting, pulling and twisting, and because the material did not stretch, they creased terribly and fell to pieces with irritating regularity.

Savile Row and the great British tailors who prided themselves on being the very best in the business did not come up with an alternative method, although some mass manufacturers did try lining ties with rubber in the early 1920s in an attempt to overcome the problems of inelasticity and wrinkling. But it took a

Above: A distinctive set of gentlemen's fashion accessories for the baseball enthusiast by Gallery of St James's, London.

Below: Macclesfield silk club and school ties, showing the variety of organizations from the MCC to Bedford Modern Old Boys that commissioned their own ties.

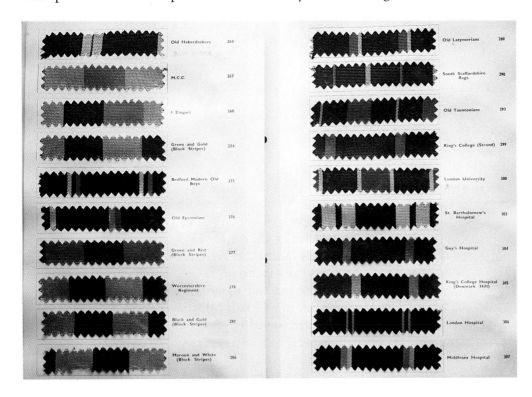

New Yorker called Jesse Langsdorf to rethink tie design and arrive at a solution which is still used today for all but the cheapest ties.

Myron Ackerman, who worked with him on the creation of what is now known as Resilient Construction, remembers the invention which made Langsdorf — a first generation American whose parents had fled Eastern Europe early in the century — into a millionaire.

Jesse had been making ties for a few years before he came up with his brainwave. Before then men had a recurring problem with their neckwear — the problem was that ties had to be pulled and tugged into place and the outcome was that they tended to fall to pieces after a short while.

Jesse simply came up with a process which meant the tie could withstand the rigors of being tugged around the collar.

Instead of cutting a tie shape straight down a piece of material, Langsdorf cut it on the bias, or diagonal, maximizing the natural elasticity of the material. The best angle of bias, he discovered, is 45 degrees, which allows the aprons of the tie to drape and fall straight from the knot. If a tie is cut off-bias it will pull off-center and fall crookedly.

THE WINDSOR STYLE

Edward VIII had such a terrific reputation as a leader of fashion that everybody has been more than willing to assume that he invented the world famous Windsor knot after he abdicated in 1936 and became Duke of Windsor. In fact, it may well have been the brainchild of his father, George V, who was photographed in the 1920s wearing a tie knotted in what looks suspiciously like a Windsor knot.

The tie knot is not the only sartorial innovation that is credited to the Prince Charming of the 1920s, but it may, in fact, have been another man's invention. A photograph of the Duke of Fife taken in 1904 clearly shows him wearing the material now known as Prince of Wales check.

Whatever the genesis of these ideas, there's no

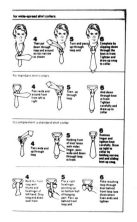

Instead of cutting in one piece, he cut in three pieces: the wide front apron of the tie, known in Europe as the front blade; the narrower back apron, known in Europe as the under-end; and the narrow part which goes around the back of the neck, known as the gusset. Each of these pieces was cut on the diagonal and with a diagonal edge, and even the interlining (or blanket) was cut in the same way as the outer (or shell) material. Then, instead of simply sewing the strips of material together and finishing the ends of each seam with a tight stitch and knot, Langsdorf introduced what Americans call the double bar-tack and the Europeans call a bar tack and a spring.

On the front blade or apron, the seam is finished with a large tacking stitch which helps to stop the material pulling apart. On the back apron or under-end, the chain-stitched seam is finished with a smaller bar tack and a loop of thread, which is pulled into the seam when the tie is stretched during wear and prevents the seam from splitting.

Jesse Langsdorf patented the process in 1924, reserving it for his own company, Frank, Strohmenger & Cowan, under the trade name Resilio. At the end of the decade, he sold rights to his revolutionary construction method to other manufacturers in the United States and other countries.

Above, above left and far left: The who, how and what of the Windsor tie.

doubt that the Duke of Windsor was responsible for their huge and enduring popularity. Suzy Menkes, author of *The Windsor Style*, claims that the Duke's Windsor knot was the product of a collaboration with his London shirtmakers, who put an extra-thick lining, or blanket, inside his ties, giving him the bulk to create the elegant conical shape of the Windsor knot.

However, although the Duke was meticulous and even inspired in his choice of clothes, his tastes were conservative by modern standards. For instance, his favorite tie was the broad red and blue stripe of the Brigade of Guards.

The Windsor knot is today favored by super-smart Europeans and South Americans. It looks best with cutaway or wide-spread shirt collars which do not cramp its bulk. To tie a Windsor knot, follow these step-by-step instructions from the Neckwear Association of America.

1 Start with the wide end of your tie on your right and extending 12 in (30 cm) below the narrow end.

2 Cross wide end over narrow and bring the wide end up through the loop.

3 Bring the wide end down, around and behind the narrow end, and then up on your right.

4 Bring wide end down through loop and cross it at right angles over the narrow end.

5 Turn and pass through loop again, and complete by slipping through the knot in front. Then tighten the knot up to your collar.

Myron Ackerman had his part to play in this classic redesign of the tie. He came up with the idea of a double-lining for the best-quality ties, using striped silk to fill in the open ends of the aprons or blades. This is now known as tipping, or French tipping when the tie material itself is used.

Female fashion trends had begun to influence the outer appearance of ties once again. The 1920s were roaring, men danced to jazz bands or shook to the Charleston with their flapper girlfriends who wore short skirts made of materials influenced by Cubist painters and Art Deco designers. And, in Paris, the

Above: The new tie department in Harrods, London, 1928. This department specialized in this most vital of clothes for men and devoted an area of floorspace to the tie almost inconceivable in modern general stores today.

couturier Jean Patou came up with the shockingly avant-garde idea of making men's ties in the same kinds of colors and patterns being worn by women.

Patou was Chanel's great rival in the world of *haute couture* in the 1920s. He pioneered the boyish, sporty look of dropped waists and slim skirts, dressing such women as the tennis player Suzanne Lenglen and the American society hostess Moira Harrison Williams, as well as Barbara Hutton, Lady Diana Cooper and the Dolly sisters. He also introduced the V-necked jersey, knitted in patterns suggested by such Cubist artists as Braque and Picasso and the Art Deco designers Louis Suë and André Mare, matched with identically patterned silk scarfs which women wore at the neck like ties.

The patterns, in greens, blues, pinks, oranges and blacks, looked so good on the scarfs that Patou decided to try them on ties as well. When he opened his sportswear shop, the boutique Coin des Sports, in 1925, there was a men's section selling these daring new designs. American women, who formed a large part of Patou's clientele, thought these were charming, and bought them as a sweetener for the men who footed their bills. Although they did not signal a mass trend, they did lead to the wide, painted, "gangster" styles which became highly fashionable in the 1930s.

It's easy to imagine F. Scott Fitzgerald's Jay Gatsby wearing the Patou style of tie, and he probably also owned many Macclesfield silk versions, imported directly from Britain. On the day that the Great Gatsby shows Daisy the contents of his miraculous wardrobe, he greets her at the door of his mansion "in a white flannel suit, silver shirt and gold-colored tie," then proceeds to overwhelm her with the wonders stored in his dressing room. Inside "two hulking patent

TIE PATTERNS

With the invention of resilient construction and the bias-cut tie, fabric specialists had to rethink their approach to designing material for neckwear.

Neither manufacturers nor consumers found ties with obviously lopsided patterns acceptable. Material now had to be printed at the angle at which it would ultimately be cut, ensuring that symbols ran vertically down the finished tie and that diagonal stripes remained diagonal instead of becoming horizontal in the final product.

The distance between each symbol in a patterned tie material also had to be taken into account. Regularly repeating patterns — also known as all-over patterns — such as polka dots did not present a problem, but any symbol or pattern which repeated at irregular intervals had to be examined so that sufficient quantities of the pattern appeared in the right places on the tie. This is known as a planned pattern.

The same problems had to be addressed in the 1940s, when below-knot patterns — that is, patterns on ties designed to have a plain knot and a large splash of color immediately below it — became fashionable.

Above: This teddy bear pattern, woven in Macclesfield silk, is an unusual example of a regularly repeating pattern.

Right: Robert Redford as the Great Gatsby in the eponymous film, wearing a gold-colored tie and collar pin in keeping with the golden age of the pre-Crash years.

cabinets" were "his massed suits and dressing gowns and ties, and his shirts, piled like bricks in stacks a dozen high." These he piles in front of Daisy, who wonders at their colors and textures – "shirts with stripes and scrolls and plaids in coral and apple-green and lavender and faint orange, with monograms of Indian blue" — and ties to match.

"I've got a man in England who buys me clothes," says Gatsby. "He sends over a selection of things at the beginning of each season, spring and fall."

Other designers, such as Charvet, followed Patou's lead and produced ties which foreshadowed the brilliant American designs of the 1940s and early 1950s, and these caught on with the young esthetes of the day. Sebastian Flyte, the beautiful, doomed hero of Evelyn Waugh's *Brideshead Revisited*, makes his first entrance in dove-gray flannels, a white crêpe de Chine shirt and a Charvet tie with a postage-stamp pattern.

THE MACCLESFIELD LONG SCARF

The recession that followed the First World War and doubled with the Crash of 1929 led to some short-lived innovations in cheap neckwear.

The most unusual of these was the revival of the Macclesfield long scarf, which had enjoyed a brief popularity in the 1860s when it had been a long, block-printed silk tie worn folded like a cravat and held in place with a stick pin.

The long scarf of the 1920s and 1930s was a very different item. Many men, who had grown used to wearing a tie and regarded one as an essential mark of respectability, could no longer afford the type of neckwear they had once favored. The mill owners of the Lancashire town of Macclesfield in the north of England came up with a temporary solution.

This was a simple length of cheap unlined silk with squared ends, or aprons, which were stamped with the manufacturer's name. Men who bought such ties would have been ashamed to be seen advertising a maker in this way, so they either tucked the offending end into their waistcoats or persuaded their wives to hem it away out of sight.

They might have been consoled if they had been told that, 20 years later, men around the world would pay premium prices to have a maker's name stamped on their ties.

Left: The Macclesfield long scarf of the 1920s and the 1930s was square-ended and made of inexpensive silk.

Above: Sir Thomas Lipton with the crew of his boat the *Shamrock IV* at Gosport. Lipton wears the tie he invented, the Lipton bow.

THE LIPTON TIE

Between 1899 and 1930, Sir Thomas Lipton was the leading light in Britain's fruitless yachting challenge for the America's Cup. Lipton, a millionaire grocer and tea-retailer, never succeeded in sailing any of his boats across the line in front of their American rivals — but he did leave them a fashionable necktie.

The Lipton tie is a bow with short, drooping aprons. It looks much like a shamrock — the emblem of Sir Thomas's native land — when it has been tied.

Sir Thomas was an elegant dresser, even while sailing, and he invented his tie to complement his yachting outfit of white flannels, dark blue blazer and cap. The tie was to be his trademark and many yachtsmen — American as well as British — adopted it as a tribute to his sportsmanship.

Above and top: Golf and cricket patterns on Macclesfield silk ties.

More conventional Europeans, led by the Prince of Wales, thought such extravagances rather vulgar. The Prince went so far as to complain that American men were too fond of loud ties, and that they mixed colors horribly, citing one American who had worn a fawn shirt, a red tie, green socks and a blue suit. Colors, he insisted, should tone, but not match to the extent displayed by another American man who had been observed wearing a plaid shirt, plaid tie, plaid socks and plaid handkerchief with — naturally — a plaid suit.

However, there were other ways of ringing the neckwear changes for these more conventional men. The sports boom which made golf a passion encouraged the wearing of knitted and woolen ties in plaids and tweed effects, and the appearance of the very wide casual trousers known as Oxford bags led to the appearance of wide, casual ties in plain poplins and cottons to balance this briefly fashionable silhouette.

Snobbery played its part, too. As the all-singing, all-dancing Twenties ran out of steam and shuddered toward the Crash and world depression, it became smart for British men who did not need to work for a living to wear bow ties in town. Their popularity was encouraged across the Atlantic as well, where early Hollywood actors such as Glenn Taylor appeared in advertisements for Spur Ties, which were jaunty spotted or patterned ready-tied bows and came with the bonus of a free booklet on movie stars called *Off the Lot*, which promised to tell "what your favorites do in private life."

Younger men found a way of irritating their elders via their neckwear. They

**Right: Leslie Howard showing
how to dress well with a striped
Macclesfield silk tie.**

**Right and far right: The
Gazette du Bon Ton of 1922,
promoting the advantages (for
the advertisers and
manufacturers at least) of
wearing conservative
neckwear.**

 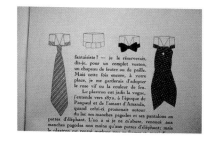

imitated the new heroes of the stage, screen and gramophone — men such as Noel Coward, who preferred soft cravats to the now-conventional four-in-hand style of tie, even in town.

Coward eventually dispensed with a collar and tie altogether and found himself a fashion leader, rather to his surprise. "I took to wearing coloured turtle-neck jerseys, actually more for comfort than effect, and soon I was informed by my evening paper that I had started a fashion," he admitted. "I believe that to a certain extent it was true; at any rate, during the ensuing months I noticed more and more of our seedier West End chorus boys parading about London in them."

But attempts to introduce anything extravagantly new into male wardrobes were doomed, both by convention and by the impending Wall Street Crash of October 1929. In the early summer of that year, British men roared with laughter at the newly launched Men's Dress Reform Party, whose stalwarts included the painter Walter Sickert and the Dean of St. Paul's Cathedral in London. They complained that menswear was too dull, preferred kneebreeches to suits, and suggested bizarre colors for everyday wear — pinks, scarlets and floral patterns among them. They were not a success.

By the 1930s with the scandal brewing over the Prince of Wales' affair with the soon-to-be-divorced American Wallis Simpson, attention was turning toward the United States — and, especially, Hollywood. Transatlantic liners were crossing the ocean and bringing the stars to Britain and British styles to the stars in a cross-fertilization which has persisted ever since.

British stars such as Ronald Coleman, Leslie Howard and Jack Buchanan were seen in movies which were deliberately designed to show American men how to dress well. The resulting passion for neckties in Macclesfield silk was just one consequence. Even home-grown Americans turned to the great tailoring institutions of Savile Row for style — with mixed results. Fred Astaire was determined to have his dancing waistcoats and tailcoats made by the Prince of Wales' tailor, but was turned away at first. Eventually he became a Savile Row idol, and the vision of him dancing in *Top Hat* in an evening suit tailored by the venerable firm of Kilgour, French & Stanbury and a white tie bought in London became the British ideal.

Bing Crosby had a more difficult time when he first visited the tailors Lesley & Roberts in London's Hanover Square. "They took one look at me and whisked me into an inner room, a cubicle in the back. I guess they didn't want the clients to see such an apparition in their shop," he remembered.

The salesman who waited on me was formal and starchy. He had on a wing collar, an Ascot tie and a cutaway. He began to lift down bolts of cloth, and, as

---

BOHEMIANS

The Bohemians of the 1920s and 1930s chose not to wear conventional ties at all, since they thought them unneccessarily restrictive. Although they had common sense on their side, they were reviled for it.

British style commentator Nik Cohn can recall the family story of his father being turned away from a café in London in 1933 because he was wearing sandals and an open-necked green shirt.

"We don't want your kind here," the doorman told him, outraged at this breach of etiquette.

Another pioneer of the open-necked look which was only to find favor in the 1960s was Royal photographer Norman Parkinson. He was laughed at in the streets for wearing an ankle-length, blood-red Harris tweed coat set off by a fetching silk handkerchief, knotted — cowboy-style — at the neck.

he unwound a big bolt, a moth flew out. Consternation is a weak word for what ensued . . . It's embarrassing to witness the degradation and shame of a brave and friendly country.

The Ascot tie witnessed by Crosby was by now an anachronism in daywear; even the Prince of Wales wore it only for formal occasions such as weddings and the Ascot races themselves. It was most certainly not the kind of tie that a new breed of male hero, imported from the United States, would have worn.

After the abdication of Edward VIII in 1936, and the succession to the throne of his quiet, conservative brother George VI, the world had had enough of British fashion for the moment. The greatest English gentleman of the era had let men down, and although in his new incarnation as the Duke of Windsor, Edward bequeathed them the Windsor knot, they were generally ready for something rougher and more masculine — which was precisely the style being purveyed by a new breed of Hollywood star.

Men such as John Wayne, the hero of cowboy movies that packed cinemas across the world, would never mess up the monarchy for a mere woman. However, the bandanna neckerchiefs he often wore were not quite suitable for everyday life. But men such as Humphrey Bogart — yes, their slouching manner, their trenchcoats, soft hats and narrow dark ties — fitted the bill very well indeed. A boom in the sales of narrow dark ties in tough and unfashionable materials such as cotton and light wool duly occurred.

Below and below right: Film stars naturally spread the fashions of the day. Humphrey Bogart wears a diamond-ended bow tie with a long-collared shirt; Top Hatter Fred Astaire in *The Belle of New York* shows off his Savile Row finery and white tie with an elongated end, an Astaire touch.

This low-life trend worried parents around the globe, who became concerned by the standards being set by such idols as Bing Crosby and the youthful Frank Sinatra who had the nerve to perform in the evenings in lounge suits and even to pose for publicity pictures without wearing a tie at all. Even Crosby's wife complained that he set a bad example to his own sons, and he admitted that his habit of lounging about in sweaters, slacks and old moccasins did not help when she was trying to persuade them into shirts and ties.

The Second World War was to break down prejudices about casual wear as completely as the First World War had destroyed the obsession with stiff collars and Ascots. Once Hitler had begun his long march across Europe in 1939, men could no longer dream of aping American styles and even Americans themselves became less ebullient.

For those who were not confined to uniform khaki or dull blue, "make do and mend" was the order of the day, and the struggle to survive overwhelmed most urges to be fashionable. Under the shadow of war in May 1939 — four months before Hitler invaded Poland — a social research project in Britain noted: "as opposed to wanting to be exhibitionist, [men] wanted clothes to make them inconspicuous."

Mass Observation was an extraordinary project set up in the late 1930s to monitor the aspirations and habits of British people. Among the myriad subjects covered by its researchers — who were known as "observers" — was neckwear. Its fascinating archive makes it clear that, for most men, ties were a welcome opportunity to exhibit personal style and that that style conveyed many messages

Above: British war hero Douglas R. Bader gets into his Spitfire to lead the Battle of Britain victory fly-past over London in 1945. He is wearing a polka-dot scarf, a fashion that has been long and widely imitated.
Below: E.H. Benson's caricature of army types, c1940, shows them wearing collar bars under their ties.
Below middle: *Boy Scout* by K. Brookes, 1943. The scarf is worn outside the loose collar and gathered in a toggle at the front.
Below right: *The Chef* by W. Orpen, 1921. The white linen scarf is well-knotted around the chef's neck: he would have used it both to wipe the perspiration from his brow in the testing conditions of his kitchen and to wipe food from his mouth as he tasted it during the cooking.

to others. One young man told an observer, "I please myself when I buy ties, ditto grey flannels. When I buy a suit or jacket, I set out to please my fiancée." Another, more conventional creature, admitted, "I don't like open shirts for games because people who wear them have sloppy minds."

But the war brought few opportunities for British men to vary the style statements they made. Clothes rationing was enforced in 1940, and few men had the neckwear wardrobe of a medical student interviewed in 1941:

> My chief variation is my tie. I have over 40 ties (I must explain that my brother has joined the forces and that I now have double my previous quota of ties, etc.) and I change these once a day or more often, according to how I feel.

There were, of course, wartime trends, spawned by events such as the Battle of Britain in 1940, when the pilot heroes of the Royal Air Force — including volunteer Americans — started wearing spotted silky cravats and scarfs instead of ties. Another fashion, which could not take root in its home country but became a great and permanent hit in the United States, was begun by the Duke of Windsor who, bowing to the rationing affecting Britain, wore an old tartan suit which had been made for his father George V in the 1890s. The British could not get hold of the material to copy him, but the Americans could and immediately began to wear tartan dinner jackets, cummerbunds, ties, bow ties and swimming trunks.

This gave Europe yet another reason to envy the United States and to yearn passionately for the luxuries that the land of plenty enjoyed throughout the conflict, even after the bombing of Pearl Harbor in December 1941 brought the Americans into the fighting. It was an envy tinged with passionate longing, one that would lead to a huge boom in demand for anything and everything American in the postwar years — and a new kind of neckwear was only one of the things that the United States was ready and willing to provide.

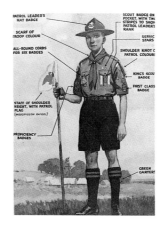

CROSS-OVER FASHION

Women took to ties when they took to trousers for their work in the munitions factories during the First World War. The sight of the "gentler sex" wearing such blatantly male costume caused considerable disapproval.

The satirical magazine *Punch* ran a cartoon in 1918 which shows a woman, with her hair tucked into a kind of mob cap and wearing trousers and a sailor-style collar and tie, walking away from an angry taxi driver, above the caption: "Taxi-driver (who has received the bare legal fare), to Lady Maud, on munitions. 'Ere, wot's this? Calls yerself a gentleman, do yer?'"

After the war, others took to a man–woman uniform as a form of desexed mourning for the lovers or husbands they had lost and could not hope to replace. For many women, marriage was out of the question because there simply were not enough men to go round. These women often dressed in a costume of man-tailored skirt suit, flat brogue shoes and collar and tie — a look still favored by some, now very elderly British women who live in the country and tramp the fields, surrounded by their dogs.

With the increasing emphasis on healthy outdoor pursuits and a fit, boyish figure, large numbers of very young women also adopted the collar and tie, especially when taking part in sports. In 1922, *Vogue* reported, "The distinction between the sexes has been discovered to be grossly exaggerated." Later in the decade, there was a brief craze for women to borrow their husbands' dinner jackets, white evening shirts and bow ties, which they wore with short, straight black skirts.

One further group of women in ties emerged when Radclyffe Hall's notorious lesbian novel *The Well of Loneliness* was published in 1928. Ms. Hall herself wore her hair cropped like a man's and affected man-styled suits and ties, which rather put off heterosexual followers of this fashion, who found the whole concept of lesbianism scandalous.

1918
Taxi-driver (who has received bare legal fare), to Lady Maud, on munitions: ''Ere, wot's this? Calls yerself a gentleman, do yer?'

From Demob to Carnaby Street: 1945–1970

Above: A wider range of designs and styles was becoming available, as well as a broader selection of manufacturing materials and standards.

The Second World War decimated Europe, winners and losers alike. There was no money, no manufacturing base and certainly no time for things such as ties when the economies of an entire continent had to be rebuilt. Even if there had been, most countries were to suffer from the rationing of all essential products and services for some years after the conflict ended.

What was more, British men who had survived in the armed services for six years wanted change. The old ways, the traditional tailoring, the muted colors — none of these matched their postwar aspirations. They wanted flash, style, color, excitement. They wanted anything and everything from America, the land of opportunity, the land which had provided the muscle to banish Hitler and his Fascists, the land which had managed to keep its GIs supplied with chewing gum and nylons even at the height of the fighting.

Europe looked West – and America was ready. The war had cut off supplies of fashionable menswear from Britain, which had, until then, continued to produce the most desirable men's clothes in the world. American manufacturers had realized that this was their big chance to take over and, predicting a longing by the returning soldiers for color and bright modern style, tie manufacturers were the best organized of all. The magazine *Arts Apparel* commented, "Europe is in no condition to design ties. Soldiers will want colors galore and they will look tie-ward for it." The great American tie boom had begun.

The trend toward the wide, extravagantly colored and patterned four-in-hand ties that ruled the world of fashionable menswear in the 1940s and early 1950s had, in fact, begun while the fighting in Europe was at its height and before the Japanese bombing of Pearl Harbor. In 1939, when *Esquire* was still advising its readers to wear ties that were "conservative, muted, an object lesson in restraint," a bizarre, Hawaiian print style of tie, colloquially known as a "belly warmer," was launched onto the American market place.

The wide, floppy tie adorned with dusky maidens, swirling palm trees and luxuriant foliage was at first regarded as a joke — although it may have been a marketing ploy for tropical vacations, or even a way for men who dreamed of taking tropical vacations to suggest that they were regulars on Waikiki Beach. However, it didn't catch on until after the United States had joined the fray and soldiers wanted to be reminded of the lifestyle they were fighting for, and be cheered up while they were doing it.

Other flamboyant styles quickly followed. There were Art Deco ties in lime green, orange, black, aqua, peach, cobalt, olive and lavender, featuring lightning bolts, sunrises, zigzags and abstract shapes. There were ties featuring Egyptian, Aztec, Mayan, Japanese, Art & Craft and American Indian designs. There were ties sporting gazelles, leopards, fountains, stylized flowers, famous buildings, popular scenes, sports . . . anything in the newly safe world that could be printed or painted on a tie was shown there, the bigger and brighter, the better.

Tie ranges, too, acquired sillier and sillier names as postwar exuberance gathered pace. One range featured motifs called "Pony Express," "Gold Rush" and "Wagon Train," conjuring up the excitement of the Old West. Another range produced by Arrow was called "Papagayos" — Papa was supposed to become so excited by his new tie that he would become happy and gay. Other thrilling ranges included "Kiss of the Sun," "White Highlite," "Crêpe Allure," "Tropical Bird Plumage," "Top o' the Rainbow" and "Cohama Sunmaker".

The trend peaked in 1946 when tie mania swept the United States. More than 600 manufacturers churned out as many ties as an avid nation could buy — some estimates put the figure as high as 220 million. Men became tie collectors, building up wardrobes of as many as 3,000 ties, and tie-swapping clubs came into vogue. One club had more than 3,500 members and 17,000 exchanges to its credit within six months.

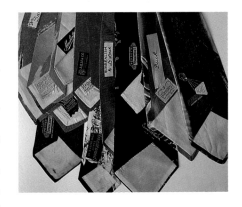

**Above: American tie manufacturers' labels of the period.
Below: Some ties reproduced from the Harrods catalog of 1948.**

THE BOLA TIE

The bola (or bolo) tie has become such an established part of Western neckwear that most people assume that it has been around ever since there have been cowboys. In fact, it is a comparatively recent invention.

In the late 1940s, a man called Vic Cederstaff rode out from Wickenburg, Arizona, to round up some wild horses in the Bradshaw Mountains. While he was galloping after them, his hat blew off, and when Vic replaced it, he decided to put his hat band around his neck, since the band had a silver buckle that he did not want to lose. One of his friends noticed this and admired it, so when he got home Vic wove a leather string and capped the ends with silver balls. Then he tucked the string through a leather band decorated with turquoise.

Soon the bola — named after its vague resemblance to the bolas used by Argentinean gauchos to bring down cattle — was being sold across the Midwest and Southwest. Vic later developed a special metal slide to take the place of the leather ring, and he patented this invention in 1959. On 22 April, 1971 the governor of Arizona nominated the bola as the official state tie.

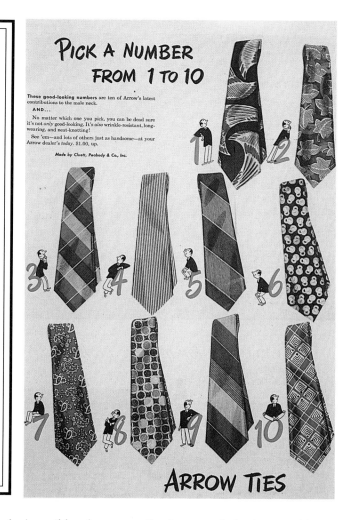

Above right: A tie for every occasion in this amusing Arrow Ties advertisement for *Esquire* magazine, 1947.

Above: An advertisement for Cutter Cravat Artist Originals ties.

"Most men like their ties wild today — a reflection, psychologists would say, of current world unrest," said the *Saturday Evening Post* with commendable understatement. "Tie cycles last from seven to ten years, so it looks like we're in for at least five more gaudy years."

Celebrities were quick to fuel the fad. Stars such as Alan Ladd and Bob Hope advertised ties, and a series called "Personali-ties" was launched. Danny Kaye, another famous collector, modeled one of his favorites — adorned with red lips and white hearts — on Valentine's Day, while bandleader Phil Spitalny was happy to talk about his 2,000-tie collection. *Good Housekeeping* told its eager readers: "Guy Lombardo orders his ties in duplicate, one for in-town, one for out. Frank Sinatra's wardrobe boasts five hundred. Sinatra often gives the tie off his neck to croon-crazy friends."

The hand-painted tie became a new cult object, and the most desirable of the genre were made by Countess Mara, who ensured that her initials appeared in every design and kept her work exclusive by making only 15 dozen of any particular style. "Tell a man you like his necktie and you will see his personality unfold like a flower," she said. At first, the tie industry sneered at what they called name-dropping, but her sales figures were so impressive that they later followed suit.

"To keep pace with the insatiable demand for ties of weird and wild designs, artists have been asked for patterns and themes for handpainted ties," *Apparel Arts* announced. Eager manufacturers hired artists such as Tina Lesser and licensed styles from French designers including Jacques Fath and Elsa Schiaparelli, to give their products added snob appeal.

FILM STYLES

The immediate postwar decades belonged more to music than to film, which generated comparatively few neckwear trends. Notably, however, there was a rash of Mexicana and string or ribbon ties following Marlon Brando's appearance in *Viva Zapata* in 1952.

The other big movie influence came at the end of the Sixties, following the release of *Bonnie and Clyde* in 1967. Fashionable men revived the old American gangster style of wearing white or light ties on black or dark shirts. This time around, though, the ties were kipper-wide.

Right: Warren Beatty and Faye Dunaway in *Bonnie and Clyde*. Made by Arthur Penn in 1967, the film accurately recreated the mood and the style of the gangster era, and encouraged a revival which soon saw interpretations of 1920s and 1930s fashions in every modish store.

Below: The gangster look exemplified in a catalog issued to celebrate the fifth anniversary of Modern Man of Carnaby Street, London. The all-black shirt is actually advertised as a 'Clyde', at 45 shillings, but the contrasting tie is not named or priced separately.

Far left tandir
St. Valentine '68's outstanding Fashion Jacket. Made in the famous **Terylene/Wool Worsted** and now presented in the **latest** Summer shades. Apple Green, Rich Tan or Navy.
Sizes: 34–40   **10.10.0**
                                    pp 4/6

And the Best News yet! It is also available as a **suit**, in either the Navy or the Rich Tan (trouser style as the Regent, page 13).
          Send an extra **4.5.0**
Sizes: 28–34W   S.M.L. Leg
Lace Roll Neck   Complete the ensemble with the latest **all lace** Roll-Shirt. A fantastic creation for Day or Evening wear. In Orange, Royal Blue or White.   **65/-**
Sizes: 14–16   pp 3/-

Capone   The Jacket you've all been waiting for! Deep **Double-breasted** pin-stripe. In either Mid-Grey, Navy or **Black**. Absolutely **no** vents.
Sizes: 34–40   **8.19.6**
                                    pp 4/6
◄   available as a **Suit** in the Navy or Black. **The fabulous matching Flares** that go with it are described on page 15.   Send an extra **3.9.6**
Sizes: 28–34W   S.M.L. Leg
Clyde   That's the **all-Black** shirt he's wearing. 'A must'.   **45/-**
Sizes: 14–16   pp 3/-

Above: Wilson Brothers
Duretwill ties.

Below: Men of Action

Such a full-blown craze could not last, and indeed, it only accounted for some 15 percent of all American tie sales even at its height. By 1948, *Apparel Arts* was noting sadly,

> In the Midwest, coin-shaped figures, controlled patterns are the best sellers. In the South, bolder patterns, lots of colors. In the West, odd combinations, while the Northwest likes California types and darker colors. The East has already taken back conservative tie styles.

But some things had changed forever. Ties were no longer seen as boring, dull essentials, and women had been quick to spot their potential for brightening up a conservative outfit. By the late 1940s, they were buying 80 percent of all ties sold by department stores and 60 percent sold in specialty shops. This gave ties a strange kind of sexual connotation that advertisers were quick to exploit. "Some like 'em shy, some like 'em neat and some like 'em big and bold!" suggested a Van Heusen advertisement in 1948. "Whatever your dish, Van Heusen has three sizes: small, medium and WOW!"

Promotions that took advantage of this female interest in male neckwear also proliferated. One of the Men's Tie Foundation's greatest successes was targeted at Valentine's Day, when stores offered women a booklet on how to tie their boyfriends' ties and another which showed how to match a man's tie to his complexion. There were even contests to choose a "Miss Valen-tie."

Father's Day provided another annual sales boost. A Botany Ties advertisement in *Esquire* in 1948 suggested, "Go farther with Father!", while Cohama's advertisement in 1950 shouted, "A Striking Promotion! Cohama puts fire into Father's Day neckwear selling with an unmatched ad 'For a Matchless Dad.'"

"Season after season, it's the number one gift item for sales," said the *Saturday Evening Post*. But after 1949, when clothes rationing was discontinued in Britain and matchless British menswear began to travel across the Atlantic once more, ties were less likely to be American.

Other factors came into play as well. The Cold War, the Korean War and a recession which began in the late 1940s all curbed the great American appetite for

Right: Wembley's 'Flower Panel' selection – seen in the January 1950 edition of Esquire magazine was created to 'mirror nature's richest colors', and cetainly gave the buyer plenty of scope to make a strong individual fashion statement.

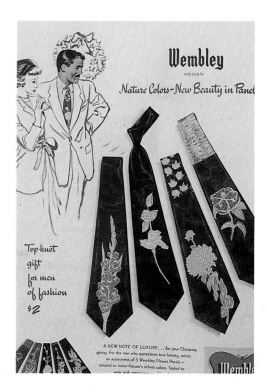

Above: Animal motifs became firm favorites with outdoor men – and sophisticates who wanted to appear to be outdoor men – in the United States in the 1940s. From left to right: Penney's towncraft ducks ties; J.B. Sax and Company's duck-shooting cene tie; the Manhattan Shirt Company's spider web's tie; an unlabeled tie featuring a faithful spaniel.

Left: Racey rat-pack style-setters Frank Sinatra and Dean Martin seen in executive mood in 1961, with dark business suits and sober ties.

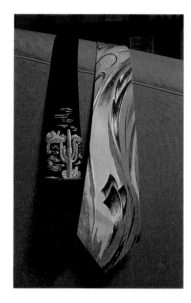

Top and above: Designs for the man who wants to be noticed, typical of the increasingly extrovert fashion style of the time. At the top end of the market, ties of the period were striking and original, but by the time the ideas and styles had been reinterpreted for mass-market reproduction, the result could be vulgar and tasteless: as the volume increased the loudness was deafening.

startling ties, while the male equivalent of Dior's New Look — a narrow silhouette, as gentlemanly as the New Look was ladylike — had brought slim, conservative ties back into fashion.

However, the glory days of the American tie industry were not over yet. In ration-restricted Britain, the sales of ties had been one of the first sales sectors to pick up in the wake of victory, mainly because a tie only cost one precious clothing coupon. But the plain woven silk or foulard ties that Harrods and other stores were selling could not satisfy the longing for color and excitement that the British had nurtured since 1939. American neckwear was clearly what the young, the eager and the plain bored were after, and the man who gave it to them founded a dynasty on his success.

Cecil Gee had owned a small chain of tailoring shops in the East End of London, but had moved to a more central site on the Charing Cross Road in 1936. Gee, a small man in his forties, had become used to more vivid, colorful and adventurous styles than most of the menswear pundits. He dressed many musicians, including Jack Hylton, but it was only in 1946, when he introduced The American Look, that he became a national fashion institution.

He stocked American-style wide-shouldered, draped suits, imported shirts with long, spearpoint collars, and fabulous ties, hand-painted with cowboys and Indians, airplanes and any other popular symbols culled from transatlantic iconography. "After the Blitz, here comes the Ritz," said Gee, who acquired the nickname Mr. Swish as a result. The effect was, to conventional eyes, rather flashy, but it was also rakish, masculine and confident — everything the glamour-starved British longed to be — and men went wild for it.

"The war had changed everything," Gee told British style writer Nik Cohn two decades later.

> Everyone had been in khaki, cooped up until they were sick of it. So when they got out they went a bit mad. Before they were called up, they might have been as conservative as anything. But now there was no stopping them.
>
> It wasn't like today, when everything is taken for granted. In the Forties, when you bought a new shirt or tie, it was a great event. A new lease of life.
>
> On Saturdays, I'd take a look outside and there were customers stretching down the road. I had to let them in six at a time and lock the doors behind them. Then serve them and let them out and let in another six.

Gee was the first British designer to think in terms of the mass-market man — "The Man in the Street," as he put it. "Until I came along, no one gave him a thought."

Other stores rushed to copy Gee's cheerful, strong designs — and to make them even stronger. Gee's comparatively subdued tie motifs were succeeded by vulgar nudes and unsubtle copies of American originals in badly printed, cheap synthetic fibers. By the 1950s, the style had acquired delinquent associations and was favored by "spivs" — black marketeers and minor crooks who were also called "wide boys," after the broad silhouette of their American-styled suits and their wide American-style ties.

Other changes were percolating through both British and American society. The young were becoming restless. They did not want to turn into mini-adults as soon as their voices broke; they wanted fun, they wanted an individual identity, they wanted their own styles to buy with the money they were earning in the postwar jobs boom. The teenager had arrived.

In the United States, teenagers meant rebellion, blue jeans, black leather jackets, T-shirts and — perhaps — a bandanna knotted around the neck. There was also a college style, for the conservative preppie, but ties weren't crucial.

SYNTHETIC FIBERS

The huge industrial and technological boom of the postwar years brought better and better synthetic fibers which were hailed for their crease-resistant and washable qualities.

In the 1940s, rayon (already popular in the 1920s) and Dacron ties began to compete even more effectively with silk in the mass market, offering men who could not have afforded a range of silk ties the chance to own dozens of hand-painted, high-fashion neckties. Firms such as Botany were pleased to advertise "wrinkle proof" ties, which they claimed would "hang-out" overnight, while Superba boasted of their "new miracle tie." "Soilit! Never Fear," said the advertising campaign. "Washit! Never Needs Pressing!"

By the end of the 1950s, new blends of synthetic fiber and wool were coming onto the market in interesting textured and knitted materials. One advertisement boasted of "New Nubby Neckwear Fabric," otherwise known as "poodle cloth" because of its curly finish.

In the 1960s, synthetic fibers in new mixes of nylon and polyester became extremely popular, even among men who could afford silk. They were especially favored for short-lived fashion fads such as the lace jabots of the Regency Revival, which were far more likely to be made of nylon than of cotton or linen thread. "Silk ties always look smartest," conceded Rodney Bennett-England in his book *Dress Optional*. "Silk is, however, expensive, and many of the ties in man-made fibers look extremely smart, clean easily and tend to give better wear."

Tie manufacturer Hans Wallach, managing director of the British firm Michelsons, agreed. "Man-made fibres are vastly superior today," he said. "They are washable and crease-resistant and as near as possible to the natural fibre. The price is the big thing. The cheaper non-silk ties now are one hundred times better than non-silk ties before the war."

Fashion also played a part in introducing new materials to neckwear. Leather came from rock stars, while the 1960s craze for crocheted dresses for women led German designer Katja Lohmann to try crocheted kipper ties for men. They were an immediate hit and were stocked at Heals in London and Bloomingdales in New York.

With Sixties fever still in their blood, the British Tie Manufacturers' Association ran a competition asking entrants to design a tie for the 1970s. They must have assumed that this would be even more sartorially adventurous, since commended entries included ties with zips, ties in overlapping layers of different materials and a transparent tie filled with colored beads.

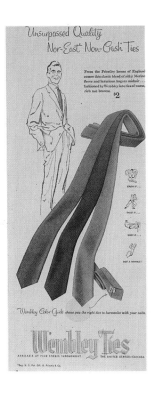

Left: The Good Grooming Leagues set up by traditionalist manufacturers attempted to combat the popularity of the more exciting designs that were becoming available by accentuating the conservative virtues of understatement and quality. Advertisements from Esquire in October 1949 (left) and October 1956 show Botany and Wembley appealing to the 'square' college boy.

The manufacturers tried to strike back, setting up a Good Grooming League to "do an educational job on High School boys" — but every good teenager knew what sort of a kid joined that. Nerds joined Good Grooming Leagues. Nerds wore geeky bow ties and synthetic fibers in dumb colors. No teenager wanted to be a nerd. He would only wear a bow tie to a college formal, and any other kind only when he had to.

In Britain, imaginative cults for the young gained ground fast. Perhaps because Britain had always been a class-ridden society where social status was expressed through dress, these early cults each had carefully defined dress codes which indicated who you were, where you came from, and what you wanted out of life.

The New Edwardians of the 1950s, for example, took their style from Savile Row. These young army officers and men-about-town wore narrow, beautifully tailored suits that buttoned as high as those their grandfathers had worn in the early years of the century. Brocade waistcoats, bowler hats and immaculately knotted silk ties were all part of a look that writer James Laver interpreted as saying, "I wish I could go back to an era when men of my class had all the advantages . . . a man-servant like Jeeves and an income from investments, which, if small, was assured."

Another subculture of dandies was more intellectual, led by the brilliant young writer Kenneth Tynan, who dyed his hair, wore gold satin shirts, purple doeskin suits, flamboyant cravats and carried an umbrella tied with a red ribbon. His look said, "I am young, I am fed up with dreary restrictions, and I don't give a damn who knows it."

Then came the Teddy Boys or Teds — working-class kids who suddenly had money in their pockets from all the jobs needed to fuel the postwar revival. They created their own version of New Edwardian style. They wore long, loose jackets with narrow, tight trousers, huge crêpe-soled shoes, and ties that were either narrow and square-ended, like early four-in-hand Oxfords, or tiny loops of string or ribbon, like late Victorian Byron ties.

They were tough, menacing, and hung around in gangs in dance halls and on street corners, where they would preen their greased hair and show off the suits they had had hand-made by backstreet tailors. Their style screamed, "So what if I'm young, working class and rough. I've got my own look, and anyone who wants to argue with it is looking for a fight." Thanks to the Teds, bootlace ties became associated with hooligans.

Bill Haley and the Comets, "Rock Around the Clock" and the start of the rock 'n' roll explosion should have given the Teds their finest hour. They had been dressing like Elvis — well, pretty much like him, anyway — for years. But they attracted millions of imitators and their style was watered down to include tight blue jeans worn without a tie. Their heyday was over.

Meanwhile other subcultures were forming and re-forming, each with a distinct and individual attitude to neckwear. From the bohemian Left Bank of Paris and the wide open spaces of America came the arty Beats, who did not see the need for such a pointless piece of clothing as the tie, and wore black turtlenecks instead.

From provincial British universities and colleges came hordes of earnest young individuals whose duffel coats or tweed jackets and woolen ties marked them out at ten paces. John Braine's novel, *Queen of the Distant Country* (1972), describes these "intellectuals" of the late Fifties wearing "coloured shirts, woollen ties, tweed jackets, flannels . . ." This uniform proclaimed: "I am a serious person. I want to change the world," and its wearer was found at Ban the Bomb marches and meetings. Braine's narrator's cousin Maurice, who is a teacher and therefore not an "intellectual," is obviously a nerd: "His shirt was white with a separate

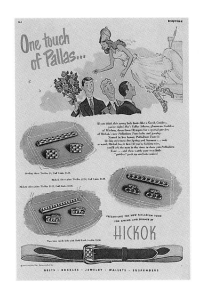

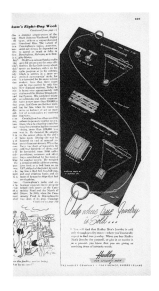

Top: 'One touch of Pallas' from Hickok.

Above: A range of Hadley accessories, 'Only where true jewelry is sold'.

Left: A Teddy Boy immaculately attired from his oiled quiff to his brothel-creeper crêpe-soled shoes. The bootlace or string tie was an integral part of a uniform that consisted of a working-class 1950s *pastiche* of Edwardian 'toff's' garb.

Above and below: Patterned and more brightly colored ties were generally accepted, even among professional groups and executives, while, right, the British establishment soldiered on with regimental and club ties, such as this range in Marylebone Cricket Club and Lord's (cricket ground) livery.

collar and his tie was patterned rayon." So much for poor, conventional Maurice. Of course, he wasn't alone. Youth cults had not yet risen to influence the mass of men in their twenties and over. Most of them continued to worry about getting things right, just as their parents and grandparents had done. In *Clothes and the Man: A guide to correct dress for all occasions*, Sydney D. Barney suggests suitable tie wardrobes for three different types of man. The "company chairman" should have 48 ties and six scarves or cravats; the "up-and-coming executive" needed a mere 24 ties, plus one cravat and two scarves; while the "bachelor in his 20s" should have 36 ties, three cravats and one scarf. These could not be just any old ties — most definitely not. "More than by any other single item of clothing the choice of a tie or bow expresses the character of the wearer," warns Mr. Barney.

It is the departure from the unwritten rules of neckwear that distinguishes one man from another. Neckwear is intended to cement the harmony of all other garments, to give the most pleasing effect to the whole outfit. It should tone but never clash. Its colour need not match nor have any direct relation to any other items of apparel, but it must be complementary. It should not distract from the face, and because it is the most prominent item of clothing, it must always be carefully presented.

As if that was not enough to ensure that the millions of Maurices around the world remained hidden behind their patterned rayon, Mr. Barney has further dire warnings for the unwary tie-wearer.

Avoid novelty ties — they are made for those who depend on the tie for conspicuity. Club, school or regimental colours are suitable for most occasions provided they are maintained in good condition. Many men, however, have the impression they may wear their colours long after the tie has passed its prime.

And not even club ties were entirely safe: "A club tie should not be worn when wearing the crested blazer of the same club."

The Italian look which hit Europe at the end of the 1950s might have been more to the staid Mr Barney's liking, with its bum-freezer jackets that made men look like waiters – until the meanswear chain stores got hold of them and made them longer and softer, pairing them with narrow trousers and very skinny ties. Narrow ties with matching handkerchiefs were an American innovation of the 1940s that suddenly found favor with Europeans at this time as well.

But it was not until the 1960s — when the Chelsea Set took over London, England began to swing and Carnaby Street was the place to be — that any new mass-market looks developed to recreate the excitement inspired by the Americans after the war.

Mainstream male fashion continued much as always throughout this hectic and revolutionary period, when dressing up, rather than merely getting dressed, was the thing to do. Ties, lapels and trousers might get narrower or wider — the three balance each other, and tend to change in concert — but a suit was still a suit, even if it was made of velvet.

The decade did make lasting changes. It underlined the fact that attitude and approach — even age — were more important than breeding, education or class. As James Laver wrote in *The Outfitter* in 1966: "The long reign of Gentility is over . . . A man no longer feels it necessary to show by his clothes that he belongs to a certain social caste. The way is open to every kind of innovation . . . " Others,

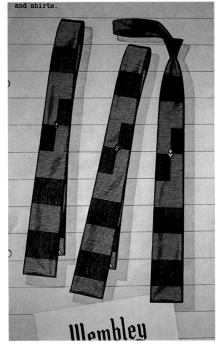

Above: Three strongly graphic Wembley ties with muted colors.

Left: A Macclesfield 1960s silk pattern.

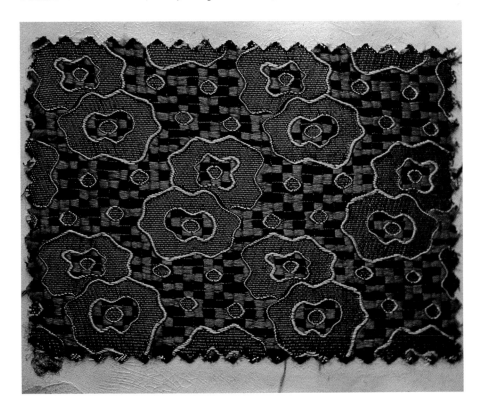

This page: Ties of the time, including, top, square-ended styles and, below, designs from Hermès.

more involved in the youth movement, felt more strongly. Sir Mark Palmer, ex-Eton schoolboy, told fashion journalist Rodney Bennett-England:

> Fashion is always a thing of the mood of the time — it's an expression of the time. The new morality doesn't really affect clothes . . . People just think for themselves . . . The colour in dress is the emancipation of the soul.

This pointed to the other major legacy of the 1960s. The riot of cults and trends and the emergence of a distinctive youth culture helped to reintroduce into every part of male costume colors and materials which had for generations been considered too feminine or *outré* for a man to wear. There was a new dandyism in the air, and London shops such as I Was Lord Kitchener's Valet became places of pilgrimage for the young of all countries, who arrived to buy old military uniforms and lace cravats — which were part of what was, for some reason, described as a Regency Revival.

Designer and all-around "bright young thing" Christopher Gibbs, who described himself as "a gentleman aesthete. But . . . a bit grubby as well; a dandy with bitten fingernails," popularized velvet ties — a trend which has remained part of evening dress wear, teamed with a dinner jacket, ever since. Even young Royals such as the Queen's photographer cousin, Patrick, Earl of Lichfield, became fashion-crazed and wore garments which would have been well known to their relatives some centuries in the past. Lichfield's major contribution was a splendid white shirt with large sleeves and a ruffled neck held together by an *Incroyable* cravat with a huge bow.

There was also a brief revival of broad ties inspired by the big American hits of the 1940s. Now, however, these tended to be painted in gentle, pastel colors and to feature rainbows, clouds and other swirling scenes instead of the original stark geometrics in strong shades.

The men who popularized these styles hung out in trendy coffee bars and bistros across London, chatted up girls in Mary Quant's ever-shorter miniskirts and worked as little as possible at the most glamorous jobs — writing, film, television, journalism, photography, design.

Their working-class counterparts were Mods, who grew from a small number of young men who affected Victorian dress, complete with frock-coats and silk cravats, to encompass a large mass of kids in neat mohair suits, Ivy League jackets, jeans and polo shirts, slip-on suspenders and knitted ties similar to the ones once deemed suitable only for golf or the country. Only their ties had any far-reaching effect. A few of the artier snappy dressers — who were at that time being watched and photographed by magazines from around the world — took them up, often in silky knits, and made them acceptable.

By the mid-1960s, England was swinging, men like Bennett-England were proclaiming that "London belongs to the young," and *Life International* had descended on the city to cover "The Spread of the Swinging Revolution," sub-titled "Even the peers are going 'mod.'"

> Now the frills and flowers are being adopted in other strata of British society, and the male fashions born in London have joined the theatre among the British exports that aren't lagging. The way-out styles already have appeared in such disparate metropolises as Paris and Chicago and may eventually change the whole *raison d'être* of male dress.

In fact, very few of the trends spawned in London had any far-reaching popularity. One exception was the first truly original necktie style of the decade — the kipper tie.

Its creator was Michael Fish (although some contemporary designers

LORD LICHFIELD

Lord Lichfield's attraction to the more elegant of the bizarre fashions of the Sixties was a boon for both the press and the mass of British men who were used to taking their sartorial lead from the Royal family. Prince Charles was too young to be much use as a fashion leader. However, Patrick Lichfield was just the right age; as a photographer, he worked in one of the new glamour professions; and he was, after all, the Queen's cousin.

He was the ultimate spokesman for the new dandyism and the clothes obsession which swept the world in the 1960s, and he admitted that he spent a fortune staying in the forefront of the movement. He told the *Observer* newspaper that he owned 26 suits (mostly brown, with tweeds for the country), 50 shirts, 50 ties, four suede coats and a huge number of turtleneck sweaters in greens and beiges which needed a lot of cleaning.

When he went shooting, he wore bottle-green corduroy kneebreeches.

The cost of such a wardrobe would have been around the then extravagant sum of £500 ($1,200) a year, if male model Ted Dawson was to be believed when he cited this as the price of owning 30 suits, 14 jackets, 75 shirts and 100 ties.

"A man should enjoy his clothes," argued Lichfield.

A man doesn't dress for himself. He dresses to attract the girls . . . I have an idea all men dress to be sexy like cock pheasants in the mating season. I always dress more carefully the first time I take a girl out than the second. English girls, I think, are more adventurous in their tastes than girls of other countries and they admire adventurously dressed men.

Left: The Earl of Lichfield was one of the last members of the Royal family to have a genuine role in determining popular style (rather than a limited influence on the dress etiquette of an élite section of the community) though Princess Diana has proved a glorious exception in recent times.

Above: The cartoon Paul McCartney sports a highly animated yellow and red kipper in Yellow Submarine (1968), proving that even two-dimensional characters sometimes get dressed in the dark.

Below: In the 1960s pop stars took the place of the aristocracy as gatekeepers of the new fashion, arbitrating taste for a generation that now looks back through its photo-albums in an anguish of embarrassment.

nominated Pierre Cardin as its real source), who worked for the Royal shirtmakers Turnbull & Asser. The tie shape he invented — the kipper (Mr. Fish had a punning sense of humor) — was enormously wide, long, and featured a huge knot and ends which always flapped (tie pins were too retro for the Sixties and, in any case, would have looked ridiculous against the kipper).

The effect of the kipper did not stop there. On its broad expanse, colors and patterns that would have been thought too feminine and effete — small pastel flowers in Liberty prints, pretty chintzes and glorious psychedelic abstracts in strong colors — somehow seemed right. Anything less would have got lost, and a plain kipper would have looked more like a baby's bib or a false shirt-front than a tie.

Even older men, whose wives were prompting them to become a bit more with it, succumbed to the allure of the kipper tie. It updated a dreary old suit nicely; it was a mass fashion, which meant that nobody would accuse them of being a homosexual; and it was so big and bold that it had a certain rakish appeal, despite its itsy-bitsy patterns. An executive could wear a kipper tie and let his boss know that he had his finger on the pulse of the young scene without risking his job; a provincial man could feel that he was hip without at the same time feeling ridiculous; parents could persuade their little boy to wear a kipper and look cute because he was pleased at the dressing-up style, instead of cross at being strangled by a dumb old necktie.

The hippies and their style were another matter. They were an international movement that grew out of American communes and the anti-war spirit of the Vietnam generation — along with, it must be said, a certain liking for mind-altering substances generally regarded as illegal and not at all a good thing, which was how the authorities tended to regard the hippies themselves.

They promoted a style that was a non-style — a defiant gesture at a society which they felt had grown too hard, self-seeking and materialistic — along with love, peace and drugs. Ties were far too conventional and conservative for their liking, but they did enjoy draping themselves with necklaces, beads and floating Indian silk scarfs, all of which were taken up by less adventurous young men as suitable party clothing and a way of irritating their parents. As a way of dressing, it was magnificently anti-taste, anti-etiquette and theatrical. A mane of long hair, half a dozen streaming silk scarves and ten strands of beads, all jostling for position around the neck, was the antithesis of the Wall Street/Brooks Brothers/Savile Row ideal of the middle aged.

At this point, the fashion explosion of the 1960s began to run out of steam. There were too many choices, there was too much confusion and the high priests of fashion were becoming downright silly, making floaty chiffon mini-dresses for men such as Mick Jagger to wear.

One comparatively respectable style that emerged from the hippie maelstrom, however, was the Nehru jacket – a long, fitted jacket with a high, stand-up collar which was worn buttoned up. The style, influenced by the obsession with all things Eastern and named after the great Indian prime minister, was a favorite with young men who wanted to show that they were *au fait* with modern trends, but who didn't want to abandon conventional dress entirely. Those who wanted a flamboyant finish to their outfit would wrap a bright silk scarf or handkerchief around their necks, leaving the gauzy material to peep through the collar slits.

It was not entirely obvious at the time. Many trend-setters truly believed that men's clothes would become more and more outrageous, that suits, collars and, especially, the useless tie would soon vanish from the face of the earth. It was a question which preoccupied Rodney Bennett-England when he interviewed a series of menswear designers for his book *Dress Optional: The revolution in menswear.*

Left: Mick Jagger, by no means the first or the prettiest of the 1960s cross-dressers, struts his Laura Ashley in Hyde Park. If dress for success is smocked frocks and flowing locks, the boy should go far.

A few pundits, such as the bizarre Texan, Ramon Torres, who designed for Harrods' new Way In boutique, gave predictably Sixties answers. Prophesied Torres:

All articles of clothing that only tradition can defend will disappear. Nineteenth-century concepts of 'elegance' will crumble — together with the very words or phrases, written or spoken, that have served so long to describe and sustain it.

Blind Bond Street, resting Rome, placid Paris, specialized New York — how wide will our ties be in 1980? How tight will we wear them? Will it still be elegant to wear a head above a stiff white collar or will we have choked it off by then?

No. There will be neither ties nor collars in 1980!

ROCK STYLES

The pop and rock explosion influenced enormous numbers of young men in the 1950s and 1960s and popularized a huge range of styles. The new stars sold image as well as music, and plundered regional ideas, designer high fashion and grandma's dressing-up trunk with all the abandon of small children creating an outfit for a fancy dress party.

At first, rock styles were reasonably conventional. Bill Haley and the Comets favored dinner jackets and bow ties, although they did spark off a brief rage for matching plaid ensembles. Groups such as Frankie Lymon and the Teenagers and Buddy Holly and the Crickets followed in their footsteps. The young Elvis Presley wore string ties or narrow four-in-hand styles with his jeans, and was copied by his fans.

When the Beatles blazed onto the scene in 1962, their manager Brian Epstein ensured that they did not frighten the grown-ups by dressing them in matching collarless Pierre Cardin suits and narrow dark ties. Suits with matching narrow ties became the pop uniform of the early Sixties, and even Jimi Hendrix wore a stylish plantation tie with a dark jacket for his early performances.

However, as the decade wore on, styles became stranger and stranger. Leather, ribbon and whipcord string ties were promoted by country-influenced rock bands such as Bread and The Band; flashier rockers such as Cream took to wearing matching satin suits and bow ties, which featured on the cover of their album *Goodbye*; proto-hippies such as Marc Bolan of T Rex wore the inevitable drooping silk scarves; folk singers such as Donovan took to lace and ruffles — and as each style appeared on stage, hordes of eager youngsters rushed to imitate it.

By the turn of the decade, Elvis, the King himself, had arrived at a costume that would be seen on disco dance floors all around the world: shiny, wide-lapeled suits with flares, balanced by a scarf knotted cowboy-style at the neck, or even, occasionally, a vast kipper tie. The Seventies and glam rock were beckoning.

Above: Britain's 'Fab Four', The Beatles, endeared themselves to their fans' parents with a clean cut image which included standard four-in-hand ties with their specially designed 'Beatle-cut' suits.

Left: Elvis Presley wearing the neckerchief that became one of his trademarks: his espousal helped to keep this somewhat antiquated style alive for another generation.

Far left: Bill Haley and the Comets, on tour in England in 1957, favored souped-up dinner wear.

Downtown   A magnificent **deep-
collared** wide stitched shirt. In three
glorious shades. Lime, Lilac or Gold.
One word for it: **Fabulous.** ▶ **55/-**
Sizes: 14-16   pp 3/-

The Polo Shirt   New! New! New!
In Green, White or Blue. **Again** fan-
tastic value and **Top** Fashion!
Sizes: 14-16½   Only **39/6**
                              pp 3/-
Plus! The **Jumbo Lace** detachable
neck-piece—White only   **16/-**
                              pp 1/-

Flower   Brilliant, shattering. In Red
or Green. **At the Year's most fantastic price.**   Only **39/6**
Sizes: 14-16½   pp 3/-

**Above: The Modern Man
catalog marketing one of the
most fantasically anachronistic
and unlikely revivals of all time
– the 'Jumbo Lace detachable
neck-piece' – providing a direct
link between the 1960s dandies
and their Regency forebears.**

**Above right: The logical
conclusion of the break-down
in conformity was the anti-
style and fashion nihilism of the
hippies: anything went as long
as it was totally dissociated
with anything that had gone
before. The tie had died: long
live the tie-dyed.**

But the majority of even the trendiest designers were more sanguine. Ties would stay, they said almost in unison, ties and the formal outfits they complemented. "Ties can brighten up a male costume and allow the wearer to express his personality," said Pierre Cardin, who claimed that he had invented the flowered tie and was to become the designer with the largest influence on the designer tie market of the next two decades through his massive licensing operation.

American society designer John Weitz believed that disposable paper shirts would be a big trend in the future, predicting that clothes would cease to convey important symbolic messages. But he was sure that ties would stay because they could cheer up men's clothes. He even invented a contraption he called a "wit-piece," which was really a short, straight-sided and square-ended wrapped cravat, to be worn with his futuristic shirts and loose, synthetic fiber suits.

Interestingly, only Queen Elizabeth II's designer, Sir Hardy Amies, and Douglas Hayward — a fashionable tailor rather than a fashion designer — pinpointed the direction fashion would really take. "The trouble is that most designers are not practical people," said Hayward. "Men want to wear a tie because it is the only thing that can express their personality. I don't want to get caught up in the present scene of accepting anything that's new. It will calm down eventually."

In fact, for most men it had never been that crazy. Later in his book, Bennett-England discusses the proper co-ordination of an outfit and the choice of tie in terms that would not have seemed out of place in Sydney D. Barney's 1950s manual *Clothes and the Man.*

The choice of tie, in particular, is a man's most obvious means of expressing his personality, especially when convention or employment often dictates the remainder of his ensemble. The tie is often the focal point of male dress, but it can be a disaster if it is so conspicuous that it stands out and dazzles. The really clothes-conscious man who wishes to appear well dressed always chooses his ties with care. They may certainly look colourful, but they should at all times complement the whole look.

A patterned tie may be worn with a plain shirt, but it is generally not successful or aesthetically pleasing to wear anything other than plain ties with check shirts. The same rule usually applies to fancy shirts, although it is possible today to buy ties which match the shirt or in similar designs with some kind of colour co-ordination.

Mr. Average, who might at his most adventurous have bought just such a matching shirt and tie, must have sighed with relief. Mr. Average had begun to suspect that the cool kids were making a fool of him. Mr. Average, who had for generations been told what to wear and how to wear it, and had been secure in his uniform, began to rummage through the back of his closet. Now, where was that nice tie his mother had given him back in 1961, before the world went mad?

When Britain staggered toward a lasting recession, Vietnam drained the lifeblood out of the United States and even the Beatles were breaking up, the party was clearly over. It was time to go back to work.

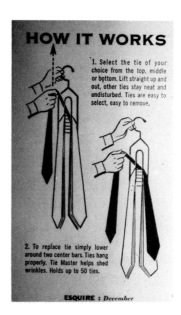

HOW IT WORKS

1. Select the tie of your choice from the top, middle or bottom. Lift straight up and out, other ties stay neat and undisturbed. Ties are easy to select, easy to remove.

2. To replace tie simply lower around two center bars. Ties hang properly. Tie Master helps shed wrinkles. Holds up to 50 ties.

ESQUIRE : *December*

TIE PINS AND CLIPS

Tie gimmicks and gadgets multiplied in the wake of the American tie craze of the 1940s, and men collected whole ranges of accessories to set off their most treasured ties.

Tie pins and clips were extraordinarily popular, and came in a stunning range of colors and designs, among them masks, bowling pins, guns, crowns, elephants, dolphins, penguins, lions, love knots, initials, seahorses and feathers. Both precious and base metals were used, often adorned with precious and semi-precious stones. Pearls, lapis lazuli, obsidian, jade, hematite, diamonds and agate were all popular. Kresiler Craft even invented a synthetic stone which would change color, like a chameleon, to mirror the tone of a man's shirt or tie.

Wily manufacturers, who knew that women bought the vast majority of ties and were always on the lookout for a gift for the man who had everything, also came up with gadgets to keep a prized collection in pristine condition. The most lavish of these was the Tie Master, which was available in a gold-plated finish and was intended to appeal to the executive running out of ideas for presents. "Looking for the perfect tie rack?", asked the advertisement. "A practical yet different Christmas gift . . . Tie Master answers all your gift needs both to clients and employees! . . . You'll be amazed at the shower of 'thank-yous' you'll get."

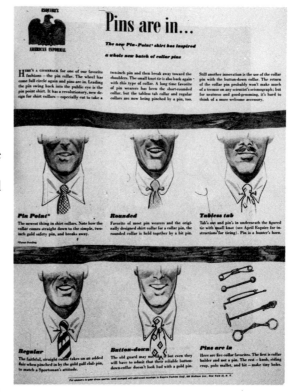

Above: Esquire magazine, May 1940: 'The new Pin-Point shirt has inspired a whole new batch of collar pins'.

Your Most Important Status Symbol: The Tie Today

Above and below: Patterned ties from the 1970s.

Regency dandies, Victorian etiquette writers and the proud wearers of regimental ties in the 1920s all knew that ties were more than a piece of material strung around a man's neck.

During the Regency in England, the properly starched and beautifully arranged cravat told onlookers that here was a man of fashion and leisure who, having money, had the time to complete the complex tying of a cravat to perfection. In Victorian England, ties became marks of social status in a class-ridden world, and a man in a brightly colored made-up tie was instantly pronounced an *arriviste*, while his neighbor in a somber Ascot held in place by a quiet pearl pin was seen to be a gentleman. And in the decades between the two world wars, a regimental tie announced, "I may have lost my money in the Crash, I may not lead the gentlemanly life I once expected, but I fought for freedom and my country. I am a man of probity."

However, the wild social upheaval of the years following the Second World War had confused these messages. By the end of the 1960s, men were no longer sure what they wanted to say with their neckwear.

Was it still smart to be seen as respectable, hard-working, trustworthy — which meant wearing a club, school or regimental tie of some description? Or was it better, in a climate where youth was idolized, to show that your finger was on the pulse of the current scene — which meant a wide flowery or psychedelic tie? Or perhaps, since these hippies seemed to have something of a point with their emphasis on caring and non-violence, was there a case for following their lead and not wearing a tie at all?

The social revolution of the 1960s had left men with almost too much choice and no firm guidelines. The glam rockers of the early 1970s did not offer a realistic option, with their crazy spangles and outrageous makeup. Cinema was in the doldrums, and Paris couture was dead — the boy wonder, Yves Saint Laurent, had said so. The booming Western economies which had fueled so much excitement and change were no longer booming, and men wanted to be told what they should wear to give themselves the best chances in life. They needed a new guru — and they got one.

In 1975, New York image consultant called John T. Molloy published a book called *Dress For Success*. It signaled the end of an era of uncertainty. It told men everywhere that being well dressed was a good thing again, that making money was a valid goal, that your clothes might even help you to become rich and happy. And its pivotal chapter was entitled "How to pick your most important status symbol: your tie."

"The tie is a symbol of respectability and responsibility," said Molloy.

It communicates to other people who you are, or reinforces or detracts from their conception of what you should be. While the most appropriate tie, worn correctly, naturally cannot insure your success in business or in life, it certainly can — and should — give off the right signals to keep you from being regarded as a no-class boob.

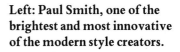

Top, above, and below: The inimitable style of Hermès.

Left: Paul Smith, one of the brightest and most innovative of the modern style creators.

Molloy had even done his homework. He had run a series of experiments that showed that men who wore ties were more likely to be seen as trustworthy than men who did not, and that they were also perceived to be better off financially than their bare-necked brothers. He had even sent a group of men for job interviews: the ones who wore ties had all been offered positions, while the ones who did not had been turned away.

What was more, Molloy even came up with a set of rules for the men of the 1970s. To be a success, he warned, a man must take tie-buying and wearing-seriously, and he should never let anyone else choose such an important item of clothing. Length, width and the materials from which a tie should be made were also prescribed. The tie should reach a man's belt buckle; its width should harmonize with the width of his jacket lapels; and the best materials were, first, silk, then imitation silk, wool and cotton.

Molloy also pinpointed the fact that the pattern on a man's tie said a great deal about his background and aspirations. "Only a few are suitable for the business-man who has reached the top or is trying to," he said. Solid plain colors were fine, even if they did suggest a man who lacked imagination. Club ties and regimental stripes conveyed the facts that he belonged to respectable social

Above and right: Ties from the modern era incorporate a vast range of influences from all the proceding periods.

Below: Extrovert and individualist, British jazz singer and *raconteur* George Melly dresses to suit his own eclectic and eccentric taste.

BOW TIES

The bow tie enjoyed a bad press through the 1970s and 1980s, unless it was being worn in the evenings with formal clothes. John T. Molloy warned in *Dress For Success*, "You will not be taken seriously when wearing one. Most people will not trust you with anything important." Even worse, he added, "In general, I have found that people believe that a man in a bow tie will steal."

Most people did not feel that strongly against it, but, apart from the fact that the bow tie has become associated with mad professors and noisy advertising men whom few wanted to imitate, it did have one very real problem: men didn't know how to tie it. It was all very well for the Men's Tie Foundation to say encouragingly, "If you were a Boy Scout wash-out and still can't do it, buy a clip-on," but men knew that readymade ties were not quite appropriate on anybody over the age of five.

A few brave bow tie fans, such as author Mario Sartori, did their best to help promote the jaunty neckwear. Sartori even wrote *The Bow Tie Book*, which came with a bright red tie and was subtitled "Learn to tie it, wear it, love it!" He suggests, "A few bow ties will make a noticeable difference in your wardrobe. They will be commented on and will make you more positive about further experimentation in achieving your own style and look."

However, most men lacked the courage or the patience, and because bow ties are now such a minority fashion, even the most fashionable of tie makers, such as Gieves & Hawkes of Savile Row, stock colored bows (for daywear only) on adjustable neckbands. "A gentleman will tie the bow himself, of course," says Robert Gieve. "But bow ties, unlike four-in-hand ties, have to be made in a man's correct collar size, and there

Above: Wembley Black Accent Bows.

aren't enough sales to justify doing this except for black or white evening bows."

The only area in which bow ties have thrived is the novelty sector of the market. Visit any joke store and you will find bow ties that light up, revolve or even squirt water at passers-by. Small boys of all ages love them.

groups and was a team worker. "Itty bitty fishy ties," featuring "some emblems of traditionally upper-class sports — a little fish with a fly in its mouth, a tennis racquet, a sailboat, a golf ball or club, a horse or polo bat" — told observers that here was a man who knew and understood such pursuits and, by extension, the rich and powerful people who enjoyed them.

Finally, there was a group of patterns — actually traditional Macclesfield silks: small diamonds, squares, circles and ovals — that Molloy called "Ivy League", signifying good breeding and education. Paisley ties were the only permissible loud ones, said Molloy, because they were the fun ties of the upper middle classes. Plaids, too, were acceptable (indicating Scottish ancestry), but an aspiring man should never think of picture or story book ties and must "avoid purple under all circumstances."

Right: Modern man can choose at will from an unprecedented range of neckwear, from the cheap to the astronomically expensive, to suit any mood, climate or social occasion.

Even at the turn of the century, the etiquette writer Mrs. Sherwood had complained that Americans were the worst nation in the world for asking questions: what did this tie mean, that color, the other pattern? Now all their questions had been answered, and they could choose precisely the image they wanted from the racks upon racks of ties on display in even the dullest local department store. American men set off on a tie-buying spree that has not yet ended.

Europeans were less certain about all these rules. For centuries, after all, they had been doing the rule-making for themselves, and some of Molloy's suggestions sounded suspiciously vulgar. A tartan tie in town? Never. But even the

British, who led male fashion since Brummell's day, saw the point. The great party that had been the 1960s was over. They had never had it so good, and now they were paying the price in mass unemployment, shrinking social services and decaying industry.

New social groups were emerging in both Britain and France, and although many people found the British Sloane Rangers and the French *Bon Chic, Bon Genre* laughable, many more envied the self-confidence and assurance of these well-connected, upper middle-class people who wore their striped silk or Macclesfield print ties like badges of rank.

The time was ripe for a new kind of tie, that would convey wealth, status, security and a familiarity with the worlds of glamour and privilege which seemed to be closed to the mass of men once more. And the big name designers of Paris were ready to provide it.

The "designer tie" — one, in the modern sense, which has not necessarily come from the studio or atelier of a famous fashion designer, but which has been approved by the star and prominently carries his or her trademark, name or initials — was perfect for its era. Men were eager to buy the positive image associated with the designer name, women loved the link with glamour, luxury and exclusivity, and the designers themselves wanted to make the money that couture was no longer generating.

The licensing concept has now revolutionized high fashion, turning men and women who were once dressmakers into society figures and billionaires who endorse everything from orange juice to car rugs. But back in the 1970s it was a comparatively new concept, and those who capitalized most quickly and effectively on the commercial value of their names became some of the richest and best-known people in the world.

Below: A handsome selection of strong designs from Pierre Cardin.

Above: Presitigious modern labels from Yves Saint Laurent and Vicky Holton.

Thanks to the earlier efforts of Patou, Schiaparelli, Fath and Countess Mara, the designers knew that ties would sell. They were an obvious first step down the licensing route, and the man who took that step fastest and most decisively was Pierre Cardin, the guru of male fashion in the 1960s and now the king of licensers, with an estimated annual turnover in excess of $2.5 billion. Although he now sells his name to the manufacturers of more than 800 different products, ties continue to be pivotal to his business empire, and a quick look at his British and American operations shows why.

In New York, Burma Bibas produce 180,000 ties every day, and between 54,000 and 63,000 of them bear Pierre Cardin's name — that is nearly 16 million Cardin ties a year. Burma Bibas, which was founded by Sam Klaus in 1926, has held the Cardin license for three years.

The deal goes like this. Burma Bibas agree to pay Pierre Cardin a certain percentage — in the United States, between 8 and 10 percent would be normal — of the wholesale price of every tie they sell that bears his name. In return, Cardin gives the company a certain number of tie designs which will account for approximately 15 percent of all the Cardin-labeled ties produced by Burma Bibas, and they top these up with styles created by their own team of six designers and approved by Cardin. In order to preserve a sense of exclusivity, only a limited number of each Cardin tie will be made in specially ordered Italian silk, usually hand-stitched, and sold in stores such as Bloomingdales, Saks Fifth

Avenue and Lord & Taylor for between $18.50 and $50.00.

In Britain, Woodstock Neckwear have held the Cardin license since 1978. They pay Cardin around 15 percent of the wholesale price of each tie bearing his name and oversee all the designs themselves — they have never had a tie design rejected by the great man. They make 10,000 Cardin ties a week, 80 percent in Italian silk and 20 percent in polyester, which are normally machine stitched and retail in stores such as Harrods, Debenhams and John Lewis for up to £22.00. Woodstock never make more than 160 of any one Cardin design.

The advantages to both manufacturers are clear. "The public recognition of the Cardin name is phenomenal," says George Camacho, vice president for sales at Burma Bibas. "If you didn't have the Pierre Cardin label, you'd find it very difficult to get people to take you seriously. If you call and say you have the Pierre Cardin label, you get an immediate access to the higher levels [of buyers in department stores]. They expect a European type of look in the Pierre Cardin label. It's a very well recognized name."

In other words, not only do Burma Bibas sell a huge number of well-respected and high-quality Cardin ties to the public, the very presence of his label among the ranges of ties they make ensures that store buyers will look at other ranges as well.

Left: One of the greatest and most recognizable labels of all — Pierre Cardin.

Right: Mrs Thatcher in a floppy bow, exemplifying her personal style which borrows heavily from the masculine while preserving a softening, and some might say disarming, stratum of underlying femininity.

Above: Two of the most closely observed pieces of neckwear in the world sit below the heads of Prince Charles and Princess Diana.

Richard Maddocks, managing director of Woodstock Neckwear, is more blunt. "People are paying for the name," he says, "The reason designer ties came about is that 80 percent of ties are bought by women and women associate or correlate designer names with couture — hence they buy designer ties.

"The quality has to be A1 and you have to keep up the exclusivity. Lots more people want to sell — and buy — Cardin ties, but we won't do it. You can buy an ordinary silk tie in a department store for half the price, but you'll know that 500 other people will have that tie. It won't have the cachet."

Not all designers license their ties in this way, although many do. Some — such as Hermès, Givenchy, Armani and Versace — keep far tighter control over design and insist that manufacturers take what they are prepared to give.

But whatever the system they use, designer ties have been the biggest innovation and success in the tie market of the last 20 years. Designers such as Cardin will have their ties produced from Tokyo to Haiti, counterfeiters from the Far East and Southeast Asia do a roaring trade in designer rip-offs, and very few men in the tie-wearing world will not have at least one designer tie in their wardrobes.

The resurgence of the work ethic, combined with advances made by the feminist movement throughout the 1960s and 1970s, meant a change in neckwear for women as well. The first generation of female executives were given their own "Dress For Success" look by John T. Molloy and his imitators, and a pseudo-male necktie was part of it.

The woman who best typified their style was the British Prime Minister, Margaret Thatcher. In her early years in power, she was rarely seen without a suit and a blouse tied in a pussy-cat bow at the neck — a man–woman's uniform which told nervous male politicians that she was really "one of the boys" and would not burst into tears whenever she was thwarted.

As women became more confident in the 1980s, they began to abandon this uniform and to play with neckwear, much as men had done for decades. Style leaders such as Mick Jagger's first wife Bianca had already shown how feminine a woman could look in a man's trouser suit, collar and tie, and executives began to adapt the high fashion look for themselves, discovering that a silk scarf tied like an Ascot or twisted at the neck could make a working suit look more feminine without losing any of its authority.

The French firm Hermès cashed in on this boom, and began to produce leaflets which showed women how to get the most out of their ravishingly beautiful — and breathtakingly expensive — silk squares, which became the career woman's equivalent of the man's designer tie.

Diana, Princess of Wales, was also a style leader in neckwear. When she first became engaged to Prince Charles, she often wore a Sloane Ranger style of high-necked, frilly-collared shirt with a narrow black velvet string tie. When she was pregnant with Prince William, she drew attention away from her stomach by wearing huge floppy Byron bows at the collars of her dresses. And when she persuaded her rather more conventional husband to become involved — through his Prince of Wales Trust for underprivileged youngsters — in the world of pop and rock music, she borrowed his tuxedo jacket and bow tie.

PREPPIES

Preppies are the American answer to British Sloane Rangers and French *Bon Chic, Bon Genre* youngsters. Although they were not cataloged by style writers until 1980, when Lisa Birnbach's *The Official Preppie Handbook* was published, their approach to clothes reveals much of the innate conservatism and self-confidence shown by their European cousins.

Their principles are neatness, attention to detail, an insistence on quality and natural fibers, and a certain androgynous, sporty look. Among their icons are ties, which have to be as classic as possible. Favorites are diagonally striped ribbed silks, club ties embroidered with shields or heraldic insignia, printed silk ties with diamond patterns, cotton Madras ties and square-ended knit ties, as are striped, polka dot and Madras bow ties.

Left: Charles and Di again, this time in the eye-catching 'his and hers' evening wear which caught the imagination of the world's style-watchers.

Above and right: The charm, style and simple beauty of Hermès.

Far right: Paul Smith's shop in London.

Each of these looks had only to be seen on the world's most photographed woman to become a cult style, and the tuxedo look for women has now become an evening classic. Once the future Queen of England had worn it, millions of other women, who might previously have thought it unfeminine or would have been put off by the velvet bow's association with *Playboy* bunny girls, rushed out to buy imitations.

Fashion for men in the 1970s and 1980s were mostly limited to casual styles and spin-offs from new youth cults. The Western look, with its knotted bandanna or bola, is now a classic for weekend wear, as are bootlace and ribbon ties for country-and-western fans. The denim craze of the early 1970s brought a short-lived fad for denim ties, and the punk movement brought a brief vogue for narrow black leather ties with square ends. But in the main, men wore the classic four-in-hand style of tie whenever neckwear was really needed.

Meanwhile, the yuppie, get-rich-quick mores of the 1980s had swept away the last of the "sharing, caring" ethics of the 1960s and early 1970s. Men were looking for brighter colors, bolder patterns and higher quality in the neckwear which was their only opportunity to ring the changes on their basic business suits. The American tie industry geared up for this by producing a handbook to help the buyers and sales personnel to promote their merchandise in the most attractive way.

The Tie Buyer's Handbook, published by the Neckwear Association of America, gives advice on choosing the best mixture of fashion and staple stock, helps out

TIE COLLECTING

Collecting everyday ties was a craze in America in the 1940s, but the fad ended with the decade. Now collectors are more likely to target club, regimental and school ties for their wardrobes, and many will travel the world to acquire famous examples.

T.M. Lewin & Sons are London's major specialist company for such ties, and stock such rare examples as the Northern Transvaal Swimming Club and the Royal Flying Corps ties, as well as sought-after lynch-pins of any collection such as the Guards regimental tie and Oxford and Cambridge university ties. There are 200 regimental ties alone, and weeding out would-be purchasers who are not entitled to buy or wear them can be a problem. The Japanese are particularly great tie collectors; individuals will spend $1,000 on bulk buys of unusual ties — if they can.

"In some cases, we do ask people to prove that they are members of clubs or are entitled to the tie they want, but in most cases there is no formal I.D. card, which can make things very awkward," says Lewin's representative Paul Symons.

"We often get chaps writing or phoning from America saying they'd like to buy a whole list of ties, which they often claim their relatives are entitled to wear. We know there are a lot of expatriate British living out there, but one man asked for ties for both Oxford and Cambridge universities, and the Royal Air Force and the Royal Navy and the Special Air Service, and it would have been very difficult for him to have qualified for all of them. We simply had to write to him and explain that it wasn't right to let him have them. It's awful if you sell your last tie to a collector and then some old soldier comes in and you haven't got one for him."

Another highly coveted tie is the Battle of Britain tie, which was designed by and is still sold at Gieves & Hawkes. Only airmen who fought in

with pricing suggestions and is a mine of information about encouraging the customer to buy as many ties as possible. Since the average American male buys a dozen ties a year, they seem to be succeeding.

"The display appeal of neckwear lies in its color, pattern, texture and feel," says the booklet. "The challenge of tie display lies in the fact that a great deal of merchandise [is] essentially the same in shape and configuration . . . "Suggestions for meeting this challenge include, "A good display must give a customer direction"; "Good display stimulates impulse purchase"; and, crucially, "Put ties in areas trafficked by women."

Far left: The exclusive Battle of Britain tie. One of the rarest and most sought-after by collectors, it should only be worn by those who so courageously maintained Britain's air defences in the war against the threatening might of the Luftwaffe.

Left: Examples of other forces ties.

the battle are entitled to wear this dark blue tie which has the rose of England and a tiny outline of the British Isles woven on it in gold. The company will only sell one after receiving proof of identity.

As the prices of antique clothing and memorabilia rise, collectors are now beginning to home in on the ties of the rich and famous as well as good examples of neckwear worn from the 19th century to the present day.

Rock and film fans are particularly keen to acquire their idols' ties, and the London auction house Phillips are selling increasing numbers. A

tie signed by John Lennon sold for around $500 in the early 1980s, and one of Elvis Presley's ties from the 1960s went on sale in 1990 for a similar amount — a lot of money for a plain black tie in synthetic fiber, even if it is fully authenticated and has been shown at the Presley Museum in Memphis, Tennessee.

"A tie that had been worn by Michael Jackson would be worth quite a bit," says Andrew Melton, head of Phillips' rock and pop memorabilia section. "But you'd have to have a certificate of ownership or a bona fide story to prove that it really had been his."

TIE FABRICS

Ties are now made in a huge range of materials, but they will normally be described simply as silk, synthetic fiber, cotton, linen or wool. Here are some of the terms for types of these fabrics and the variations in weaving and production techniques that are commonly used in modern ties.

Armure Heavy and expensive silk with a pebbled surface.

Barathea In the United States, a pebbled material in silk or rayon. In Europe, a fine wool, suitable for bow ties or informal four-in-hand ties.

Basket weave Material which mimics the weave of a straw basket. The effect is achieved by weaving two or more yarns, side by side, in each direction.

Brocade Rich, heavy material with raised figuring.

Challis Supple, lightweight wool or cotton material, either a plain weave or a twill.

Charvet Also known as Regence; a soft, lustrous material with a faint herringbone effect.

Double warp twill Material produced either with a two-threaded twilled warp with both threads of the same color or with threads of contrasting colors. Both techniques emphasize the twill.

Dusty madder Dying and finishing technique which gives normally bright silks a dusty, muted color, most often used on busy patterns such as paisley.

Faille Flat-ribbed material with a slight sheen.

Foulard In Europe, a foulard is a square of light wool or silk which may be knotted at the throat. Also a type of silk, often with a woven pattern, commonly used for modern ties.

Gaberdine Tightly woven twill with diagonal ribbing.

Grenadine Loosely woven material made of hard twist yarns with a rough, pebbly surface.

Heavy madder Heavy DUSTY MADDER is so expensive that it is used only by the finest tie manufacturers and is always cut and sewn by hand.

Herringbone Broken twill weave with a finish of alternating diagonals.

Homespun Plain woven, loose, heavy material made of coarse, uneven yarn.

India corah Light, washable silk in natural cream or off-white from eastern India.

Jacquard Method of weaving which permits the construction of complex, multidirectional patterns.

Jaspé Faintly striped material created by weaving together different shades of the same colored yarn.

Mogadore Closely woven, finely corded silk, usually made in colorful stripes.

Moiré Finishing process, using engraved rollers to press a rippling pattern into material.

Organzine Raw silk yarns made of two or more twisted singles which are then doubled and twisted in the reverse direction in the ply.

Ottoman Lustrous cord woven silk material with wide ribs. Ottoman originally came from Turkey.

Paisley Traditional Indian pattern of tadpole-like figures, a favorite for ties.

Polyester Synthetic fiber much used for making imitation silk ties and especially fashionable in the 1960s. Poly-cotton is a blend of polyester and cotton, which is more crease-resistant and harder wearing than cotton alone.

Pongee Lightweight silk of uneven yarns, characterized by nubs and irregular cross-ribs.

Poplin A tightly woven, plain material of silk, cotton or synthetic fiber.

Rayon Cellulose-based fiber used both on its own and in blends. Extremely popular in the 1940s and 1950s as an imitation silk for ties.

Rep Also repp; material with narrow ribs, made in silk, wool and mixes and usually either plain or striped.

Shantung Rough, plain weave material, originally made of silk. Nubs and slubs are purposely included to give the material its characteristic finish.

Twill Material with a diagonal weave, including GABARDINE and HERRINGBONE.

Woven In neckwear, a design which has been woven into the material using yarn-dyed thread, rather than printed on after the material has been made.

This is the reason for the apparently bizarre habit stores have of putting a rack or two of ties close to the main doors on the ground floor — often a good ten minutes' walk away from the menswear department. Women who have overdone it on the charge card may pick up a tie as a sweetener for the men in their lives, while women who simply want to find a gift do not have far to look. "Women account for more than 50 percent of all tie purchases, and it is, therefore, important that neckwear be merchandised in areas trafficked by women," says the handbook.

The Neckwear Association's work on behalf of its hundreds of manufacturing members is unremitting. Their public relations operation — which includes such promotions as "New Ties for Old," "Design a Tie for Dad," "Neckwear Parties" and "Ties of the Rich and Famous" — reaches an estimated 100 million consumers a year, and has helped to build up an annual sale of more than 500 million ties.

The other major tie manufacturers of the moment are the Italians (although their field of dominance is in producing the silk from which ties are made), the French, the Chinese (who are gearing up to make the most of their huge silk-producing capacity) and the British.

The 1980s saw a great revival of the old-fashioned, hand-made British tie in a vastly increased variety of colors and patterns. Traditional Savile Row companies such as Gieves & Hawkes sell their beautifully crafted wares to American and

Above: Prince Charles is consistently voted one of the world's best dressed men.

Left: Robert Gieve of Gieves and Hawkes, one of the most experienced, knowledgeable and authoritative tie men in the world. He is wearing a 19th-century Belcher scarf ring on his little finger.

Japanese visitors who order dozens at a time, while tens of thousands of British silk ties are now being exported to the United States every year.

President George Bush is one of Gieves & Hawkes' most devoted tie clients and has been photographed for the cover of *Time* magazine wearing one of their ties. Both Prince Charles and Prince Philip shop there, and Robert Gieve, who has helped them to choose many of their favorites, is happy to pass on his inside knowledge of what makes a superlative tie.

"First, check that the tie has been cut on the bias in three sections," he advises. "You can actually see the grain of the material if you examine it carefully. Then look at the reverse side of the tie, at the ends — the British word for them is the 'blades,' while the Americans call them 'aprons.' Look for the bar tacks on both the large and small ends of the tie, and for a little spring of thread on the small end, which will stretch into the tie while you're wearing it and prevent the stitching from snapping.

"Next, pull the seams very gently so that you can see that the tie has been stitched by hand, which gives it the maximum resilience. And pull the pocket formed by the tipping — that's the lining on the tips of the blades — so that you

Right: Modern designs allow the flexibility for strong personal dress statements without usually descending into the vulgarity or banality sometimes evident in earlier decades. In an era where normally acceptable business-wear continues to consist of a dark or at least plain suit, the tie offers one opportunity for the personality to be rigorously or discreetly exhibited.

TIE LENGTHS

Neckties vary in length according to traditional standards in their country of origin and the average height and neck-size of the men who live there.

American men tend to be tall and have large necks — their average collar size is 17 inches (43 cm), compared to 16 inches (41 cm) in Britain — but they prefer the tip of the blade/apron of their tie only to reach their belt buckle. As a result, the average tie length in the United States is between 53 and 57 inches (135 and 145 cm).

British men like to wear their ties long, with the tip of the front blade/apron reaching to the first button of the trouser fly — about an inch (2.5 cm) down the zipper. Their ties average between 55 and 58 inches (140 and 147 cm) in length.

European men from the Mediterranean countries are, in general, shorter than either the British or the Americans, and almost all Europeans prefer a belt-length tie. Thus ties made in France and Italy will usually be two or three inches (5 or 8 cm) shorter than their British equivalents.

Attempts by associations and guilds of tie manufacturers to standardize tie lengths have proved fruitless. Each country is proud of its own tie idiosyncrasies and is reluctant to change.

can see it goes well up into the body of the tie. On a good tie, you shouldn't be able to see the blanket [interlining].

"Finally, pinch up a piece of the shell material on the face of the largest blade of the tie and check how thick the silk is. Then feel beneath it for the interlining material, which is known as the 'blanket.' Sometimes manufacturers will use very thin, cheap silk and bulk up the tie by using a heavy blanket — although, of course, a good tie in a delicate material needs a heavy blanket or a double layer of interlining, too."

Mr. Gieve suggests that the best ties are made in heavy silks and twills, and he is especially proud of a range made by Gieves in a silk called "heavydustry madder," which is usually deemed too expensive for use on ties.

"Treat your ties well and they will last well," he advises. "Always smooth them out when you take them off and then hang them up so that they can return to their natural shape."

Many men today are convinced that the tie around their neck tells a watching world too much about their personality — a feeling fostered by the likes of John T. Molloy and his *Dress For Success* lists. But experts in social psychology do not often agree. Guy Fielding of the Dorset Institute in southwest England has studied the importance of the tie in modern dress and believes that the wide variety of neckwear seen in most offices and on most Main Streets today simply indicates that men are more self-confident and fashion conscious than they were in the days when only a club or regimental stripe was a safe look.

Above left: A diverse range of ties presents the opportunity to match the selection either to the mood or to the occasion – playing safe or being noticed.

"Ties are the perfect weapon in the battle between conformity and individuality," he says. "In my office, nine out of ten of my colleagues wear blue suits. We all want to say we're part of the same group. However, we also want to say 'I'm different.' The tie allows us to make both statements — I'm part of the group, I wear a blue suit, I'm different, look at my tie. It's a nice way of solving both problems."

Fielding laughs at the suggestions that the particular pattern or material a man chooses reveals more than very basic information about him. "It's absolute nonsense to say, as people have claimed Freud did, that a paisley-patterned tie

Above: A Paul Smith tie.

Right: A pair of very unusual ties incorporating metalwork in the design.

HOW TO MAKE A TIE

There are 22 steps in the construction of a modern necktie, from cutting the shell material to stitching on the manufacturer's label.

The shell fabric — the material that is seen on the face of the tie — is the biggest expense in the manufacturing process, so it takes a skilled worker to cut as many ties as possible, all on the bias, from one length of material. Ties are cut in three sections — sometimes in two for cheaper neckwear — and 33 square feet (10 sq. m.) of material should yield about 40 ties.

The interlining or blanket — the heavy lining which helps a tie to keep its shape and wear well — is also cut on the bias.

Then the outer shape is sewn together so that seams are located in the neckband area under the shirt collar. Production then proceeds from the inside out. The ends are hemmed, and tipping — the second lining which can be seen at the ends of the tie — is added.

Seams and ends are pressed into shape, and the interlining is stitched to the outer shell — by hand if the tie is very expensive, but by a slip-stitching machine in most cases.

The tie is now turned right side out, and a cardboard shape is inserted while the tie is pressed on the reverse side. Finally, the manufacturer's, designer's or store's label is sewn on the back. This may be in the form of a loop, so that the back apron, or smaller apron, of the tie can be slipped through after tying. This label may also contain

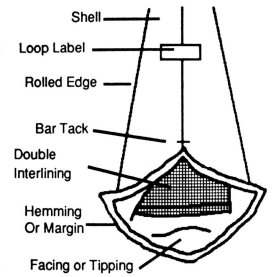

information about fiber content and country of origin, although ties are exempt from care labeling regulations in the United States.

After labeling, a bar tack stitch is often added to reinforce the slip stitching which joins the tie together.

Three machines are commonly used for the manufacture of ties. The Toni machine joins the blanket to the shell, and centers the blanket (lining) and chain stitches it to the outer shell. The Nu-Mode machine slip stitches in a zig-zag which closely simulates hand stitching. The Liba machine, a semi-automatic machine, also reproduces hand slip stitching.

signifies virility because of its resemblance to sperm," he says. "All you can safely say is that extroverts tend to like bright colours and patterns, because they're sensation seekers, while introverts like their colours to be muted."

What interests him is the cultural and symbolic significance that the tie has acquired in the centuries since it began as a lace cravat designed to show a man's wealth. "The tie has basically traveled from the West to all other parts of the earth and is worn as a status symbol to say 'We are like the rich West,'" he explains. "The tie shows that you don't have to do manual work. It's not sensible to wear a tie if you live in a hot climate either, but men still do so. It shows other people that they have occupations where they don't have to sweat and strain using their bodies, but use their minds in superior occupations instead. So the tie becomes the mark of an admired and respected group in society, and others imitate it, just as men imitated the silk cravats worn by fighter pilots during the Second World War because they were admired and respected. It's precisely because the tie is so utterly non-utilitarian that it's ubiquitous — just like Coca Cola, which is a nice enough drink but not an essential for survival. But Coke and the tie have come to symbolise the West, and they're the most pervasive icons of Western culture in the world."

Glossary

Text words in SMALL CAPITALS indicate a word defined elsewhere in the glossary.

Allover   Design, such as polka dots, which REPEATS continuously and regularly over the entire surface of a tie.

Apron   American term for the wide ends of the tie (front and back aprons) — the end of the (in British terminology) BLADE or UNDER-END.

Ascot   Wide CRAVAT secured with a stick pin, named after the neckwear worn to the Royal Ascot race meeting in England, common as business wear in the late 19th and early 20th centuries. In the United States, the word has come to mean a cravat. In Europe, an Ascot cravat is now made of pale gray patterned silk and is worn only to weddings, as very formal daywear with morning dress, and to the Ascot races. *See also* PUFF ASCOT.

Balanced bow tie   BOW TIE with two or more motifs woven so that the designs are in identical postions on each apron (blade) when the tie has been knotted. *See also* PLANNED PATTERN.

Bandanna   Also spelled bandana, bandannoe; brightly colored and traditionally patterned Indian cotton KERCHIEF, popular as neckwear for the working man from the 18th century. Bandannas have also become part of Western American cowboy folklore and fashion.

Band-bow   American term for a pre-tied BOW TIE, usually with an adjustable band which goes around the collar and is fastened by a hook.

Bar tack   Stitch made in heavy yarn to reinforce the slipstitching which joins the body of the tie at the front APRON (BLADE) end. If a tie has FRENCH TIPPING, the bar tack will join the top of the internal POCKET with the body of the tie and will prevent the pocket from slipping.

Batwing   Also referred to as batswing and, in the United States, as a bat bow; the wide BLADES of a BOW TIE, which look like batwings before tying.

Belcher   First popular colored neckwear, named after the 18th-century English pugilist who wore a wrapped and knotted blue-and-white spotted KERCHIEF around his neck. He also gave his name to a scarf ring, usually made of gold, used from the late 18th century until World War I.

Bias cut   Cutting of material on an angle, ideally at 45 degrees to the warp or weft (TRUE BIAS). SHELL material and INTERLINING for ties have been cut on the bias since 1920, when an American name Jesse Langsdorf introduced the concept of RESILIENT CONSTRUCTION to the neckwear industry. A tie cut on the bias will stretch slightly if gripped just below the knot and at the widest part of the APRON or BLADE.

Blade   British term for the broader pendant end of a modern tie, which hangs to the front when the tie is worn, or the ends of a BOW TIE.

Blanket   Also known as interlining; heavy material used as lining to give bulk and firmness to a modern tie, BIAS CUT in the same way as the SHELL material. The lighter the shell material, the heavier the blanket. Some ties will have a DOUBLE BLANKET, or two layers of interlining.

Bola   Also bolo; a novelty tie made of heavy string, braid or length of leather, capped at the ends with silver, and fastened at the front of the neck by an ornamental sliding device, often of silver or turquoise. The official state tie of Arizona.

Bootlace   Narrow cord or leather strip tie in a drooping BOW TIE, fashionable among British Teddy Boys of the 1950s. Its origins lie in cowboy fashion and films, and in the neckwear common among South American rancheros.

Bow tie   Generic name for any tie consisting primarily of a bow at the neck. The word derives from the French JABOT. The modern bow tie is a relic of the sewn-on bow which usually decorated the front of an 18th-century stock.

Butterfly   Also called a club bow; a BOW TIE shaped so that it narrows sharply at the center of the bow, which is about half the width of the BLADES. The butterfly can have pointed or square blades. *See also* PAPILLON.

Byron   The English poet Lord Byron rarely wore a tie but had several styles named after him anyway. In the 1820s, the Byron was a big floppy bow in brown, black or white. By the 1840s, it was a narrow ribbon or string tie, similar to those worn by American plantation owners. From the 1860s onward, the Byron tie was a larger — often readymade — floppy bow, sold in gents. outfitters and favored by fashionable young office workers.

Club bow   See BUTTERFLY.

Club tie   Tie in the colors chosen by a particular club or group. The first club tie is credited to the members of the Exeter College rowing team at Oxford University, who took the striped bands off their rowing hats and tied them around their necks in 1880.

Cravat   Wide cloth or piece of lace knotted or tied around the neck. The term was first used in the mid-17th century and has come, in some parts of the world, to be synonymous with an ASCOT. The cravat was the forerunner of the modern FOUR-IN-HAND tie.

Cravat string   Ribbon used in the 17th century to tie a heavy lace CRAVAT in place; the forerunner of the 18th-century SOLITAIRE.

Designer tie   Originally, a tie produced by a famous designer such as Patou, who made the first designer ties in the 1920s. Now it is primarily one which incorporates the initials, name or logo of a designer or design house into the pattern of its SHELL material — a trend started by Countess Mara in the 1940s and continued today by names such as Pierre Cardin, Gucci and Dior.

Dimple   Vertical groove under a FOUR-IN-HAND or WINDSOR KNOT.

Dog-collar   Plain band of starched linen encircling the neck and overlapping in front, introduced in the 1860s when high collars, and the high NECKTIES which surrounded them, ceased to be fashionable. In the 19th and early 20th century, the dog-collar was worn with a low, soft CRAVAT or ASCOT. Now it is only worn by the clergy.

Double bar tack Bar tacking both front and back APRON (BLADE and UNDER-END) of the tie. In the United States, a tie with a double bar tack will also have a SPRING. *See* BAR TACK.

Double blanket Two layers of BLANKET inside a tie.

Dux Stand-up collar with its corners turned down at the front, introduced in the 1860s when it was worn with CRAVATS, BOW TIES and the early FOUR-IN-HAND tie. It developed into the modern wing collar.

Facing Long TIPPING used on the front APRON or BLADE, usually in high-quality ties. Two types are used. Three-quarter facing extends 6–8 inches (15–20 cm) up the tie, while full facing ends just under the knot. Both types give an exceptionally crisp, luxurious feel to a tie.

Falling bands Also known as RABAT and hanging collars; linen or lace collars with two distinct ends hanging down over the chest. The forerunner of the CRAVAT in the 17th century, when they were worn by both men and women.

Focalium Scarf used by Roman soldiers and orators to protect their throats or as a mark of having fought in the Dacian campaign under Trajan. *See also* SUDARIUM.

Foulard In Europe, a square of light wool or silk which may be knotted at the throat. Also a type of silk, often with woven pattern, commonly used for modern ties.

Four-in-hand Originally a club formed by young English bucks who enjoyed driving and racing their fashionable horses together in the early 19th century — hence a name applied to 19th-century sporting neckwear, of which the modern pendant tie was one example. Now the common name both for a modern tie and for the knot most often used to tie it.

French tipping Lining of a modern tie, made of the same material as the SHELL and sewn to form a POCKET. *See* TIPPING.

Gros point Also known as *point de Venise* and Venetian lace; very expensive heavy lace from Venice, the most fashionable material for CRAVATS among aristocrats and royalty in the 17th century. The lace was usually held together with a ribbon or CRAVAT STRING, or sewn into a preformed bow and fall because it was too heavy to be tied accurately.

Gusset Center section of a well-made modern tie which goes around the back of the neck and joins the front APRON (BLADE) to the back APRON (UNDER-END) or SMALL-END).

Half-Windsor *See* WINDSOR KNOT.

Hand slip stitching Hand-sewing together the SHELL and BLANKET of a tie offering maximum resilience and the best draping. It is characterized by the presence of a SPRING at the end of the back APRON (UNDER-END or SMALL-END).

Hanging collars *See* FALLING BANDS.

Hemming Turning under and stitching the end of the APRON (BLADE) by machine. Mass-produced and less expensive ties are hemmed. The best neckwear is hand-rolled, its edges rolled over and stitched carefully in place by hand.

High left, low right Direction in which the stripes on British and European ties run – high toward the left shoulder running downward toward the right hip.

High right, low left   Direction in which the stripes on American ties usually run — high toward the right shoulder, running downward toward the left hip.

Hunting stock   CRAVAT of white linen or blue-and-white spotted cotton worn today by riders at fox hunts or in show jumping. The survivor, in a direct line, of the early 19th-century cravat, although its name betrays its neck-protecting origins in the 18th-century MILITARY STOCK.

Interlining   *See* BLANKET.

Jabot   Early CRAVAT of lace, often readymade, worn during the 17th century. The lace fell in a soft bunch to the upper chest and was either knotted and draped or tied in a soft bow. The linguistic origin of the modern BOW TIE.

Kata   Scarf of silk or cotton gauze given in Tibet to the priest in a temple or the host in a private house.

Kerchief   Square of cotton, linen or silk, used as neckwear among the working classes until the early 20th century. In the 18th and early 19th centuries, neckhandkerchiefs were also used by gentlemen as CRAVATS. *See also* BANDANNA.

Kipper tie   Extremely broad and often brightly colored and patterned tie introduced in the early 1960s by British menswear designer Michael Fish for Royal shirtmakers Turnbull & Asser in London. The front APRON (BLADE) of the tie was 5–6 inches (12–15 cm) wide.

Liba machine   Semi-automatic machine which reproduces hand slip stitching.

Macclesfield   Tie with small, yarn-dyed patterns consisting of small, regular, repeating symbols. Typical of the style produced from the mid-19th century in Macclesfield in northwest England.

Macclesfield long scarf   Straight-ended, Oxford-style tie, cut along the grain of cheap silk and stamped on the front of the front APRON (BLADE) with the manufacturer's name.

Military stock   High stiffened collar in black satin, sometimes adorned at the front with a sewn-on bow or drape of material. Worn by military men and sporting bucks throughout the 18th century.

Neckcloth   Term used from the 17th century until *circa* 1840 to describe either a CRAVAT, STOCK, KERCHIEF or BANDANNA worn around the neck.

Neckhandkerchief   *See* KERCHIEF and BANDANNA.

Necktie   Usual term for male neckwear from around 1840 onward, superseding the word NECKCLOTH.

Nu-Mode machine   Machine used for slip stitching ties in a zig-zag which closely simulates hand stitching.

Octagon   Readymade scarf arranged octagonally and suspended from a band fastened behind the neck; something like a modern CRAVAT or ASCOT. It was fashionable from the 1860s until the end of the 19th century.

Oxford tie   Four-in-hand tie with squared-off ends to the APRONS or BLADES. When the boat club crew of Exeter College, Oxford University, made impromptu ties from their square-ended hat bands, they inadvertently invented this style, which inspired the manufacture of numerous other CLUB TIES.

Pallium Draped cloak used in Roman times. It was folded back to give the effect of a long scarf hanging around the neck and ultimately evolved into the Christian priest's stole.

Papillon French word for butterfly, used in Europe to describe a shape of BOW TIE. *See* BUTTERFLY.

Piccadilly Stand-up collar introduced in the 1860s; the first detachable collar.

Planned pattern Pattern designed before it is woven so that the motif(s) will be positioned in a predetermined place on the tie. Under-knot designs and BALANCED BOW TIE designs are examples.

Plantation tie Also planter's tie; narrow ribbon tie, worn with a soft collar, popular among plantation owners in the Southern states of America from the late 18th century. The plantation tie is now most closely associated with Colonel Sanders of the fried chicken fast food chain.

Pocket Cavity in a tie with FRENCH TIPPING. The top of the pocket should end at least ½ inch (1.2 cm) beyond (and inside) the inverted V at the back of the APRON or BLADE.

Point de Venise *See* GROS POINT.

Puff Ascot Readymade tie mimicking an ASCOT, characterized by a bulge — often made by wadding — where the ends emerge from the knot. Puff Ascots were often sold complete with a stick pin carrying a synthetic pearl. They were popular in the late 19th and early 20th centuries.

Rabat *See* FALLING BANDS. Possibly the origin of the word CRAVAT.

Regimental stripes Authentic colors and stripes of British army regiments, used on ties. Regimental stripe ties were pioneered in the 1880s, after traditional, gorgeously colored military uniforms were abandoned in case they made too good a target for enemy riflemen. These colors were often preserved in ties. Imitations are now very popular for conservative business wear, and similarities can also be seen in CLUB TIES and SCHOOL TIES.

Repeat Interval of a pattern. For example, a 2-inch (5 cm) repeat would be a PLANNED PATTERN which repeats itself at 2-inch (5 cm) intervals.

Resilient construction Standard method of making a modern FOUR-IN-HAND tie, introduced in 1920 by Jesse Langsdorf. Important features are the bias cutting of both SHELL and BLANKET (lining) material, and slip-stitching of the two. Resilient construction gives a tie the best draping qualities and allows for easy and effective knotting.

Ruff Stiffened frill of lace or pleated linen, worn in the 16th century. A forerunner of FALLING BANDS and CRAVATS.

Sailor's tie Long tie tied in a sort of reef or square knot, fashionable in the late 19th and early 20th centuries. A sailor's tie of another sort, this time a scarf knotted low and loose around the neck, is still worn by women and children as part of a sailor suit.

School tie In the wake of the vogue for sporting CLUB TIES and REGIMENTAL STRIPES, the British public schools began to design their own school ties in the 1890s; the practice later extended to other private schools and to state schools. Schools also produced ties for different ages and abilities and for ex-students.

Shakespeare   Also Shakespear, Shakespere; a turned-down collar introduced in the 1860s. The prototype of the modern shirt collar.

Shell   The outer fabric of the tie; the most expensive and decorative material used to make the tie.

Small-end   *See* UNDER-END.

Solitaire   Narrow black ribbon fashionable in the 18th century. It was tied to the wig, then brought around to the front of the neck and fastened, usually in a bow, over the STOCK.

Spring   Loop of thread left at the end of the seam joining the back of the small APRON of hand-made and expensive FOUR-IN-HAND ties. This loop of thread is drawn up into the length of the tie during wear, preventing the seam from splitting, adding elasticity to the tie and helping it to keep its shape.

Square-end tie   *See* OXFORD TIE.

Steinkirk   Also spelled Steenkirk; long CRAVAT, often tipped with a fringe or lace, worn with one end tucked through the buttonhole or pinned with a brooch to the coat-front or waistcoat. Fashionable among men and women for several decades at the end of the 17th century and until the mid-18th century. The name comes from the battle of Steinkirke in Holland in 1692, where French soldiers were in too much of a hurry to tie their cravats properly before going out to fight.

Stick pin   Long pin with an ornamental head used to secure a CRAVAT or, latterly, an ASCOT. The stick pin developed out of the brooches used from the 17th century to secure the CRAVAT and, by the mid-19th century, had become a hugely popular fashion item. The fad lasted until the end of the First World War, after which the FOUR-IN-HAND tie became the standard form of neckwear and TIE CLIPS and TIE PINS took over from stick pins.

Stock   High stiffened collar, covered with linen or black satin and fastened at the back of the neck by strings or STOCK BUCKLES. A piece of material simulating a CRAVAT was often sewn onto the front of the stock. First introduced as military costume at the start of the 18th century, and highly fashionable for the rest of that century. Old-fashioned men wore stocks until the 1850s. *See also* HUNTING STOCK and MILITARY STOCK.

Stock buckle   Buckle used to fasten the STOCK of the 18th and early 19th centuries. Rich men had buckles of gold, silver and diamonds, even though these ornaments were usually hidden by their wigs.

Stock pin   Safety pin-shaped pin, usually in gold, sometimes ornamented with sporting designs and stones, used today on HUNTING STOCKS worn by riders.

Sudarium   Roman term for a knotted KERCHIEF worn around the neck.

Tallith   Jewish prayer shawl.

Teck   Readymade FOUR-IN-HAND, named after the Duke of Teck, a cousin of Queen Victoria. Hugely popular in late 19th- and early 20th-century America.

Thistle   Also thistling; variety of shape for the BLADES of a BOW TIE, resembling a thistle before the tie is knotted.

Tie clip   Spring-loaded fastener used to clip the front APRON (BLADE) and UNDER-END of the FOUR-IN-HAND tie together, and the two pendant ends of the tie to the shirt. Intermittently fashionable since the 1920s, tie clips may be expensive jewelry comprising precious metals and stones or cheap and cheerful joke items in base metal or plastic. They have also been used as advertising gimmicks, ornamented with club or company symbols and logos.

Tie pin Also tie tack; ornamental pin, derived from the STICK PIN used to keep a FOUR-IN-HAND tie in place, to preserve the DIMPLE under the knot, and simply as decoration against a somber shirt and tie. Materials employed are similar to those used for TIE CLIPS.

Tipping Inside lining of a modern FOUR-IN-HAND tie, seen on the underside of the pendant ends of both the front APRON (BLADE) and the back APRON (UNDER-END or SMALL-END). If the tipping is made of the same material as the SHELL of the tie, it is known as FRENCH TIPPING.

Toni machine Machine which joins the BLANKET (lining) to the SHELL. It centers the blanket and chain stitches it to the outer shell.

True bias Angle of 45 degrees to the weft or warp of the material. *See* BIAS CUT.

Under-end Also known as the SMALL-END; British term for the smaller, narrow end of a tie which hangs behind the BLADE (front APRON).

Under-knot tie Tie with a design which appears only below the knot when the tie has been tied. *See* PLANNED PATTERN.

Venetian lace *See* GROS POINT.

Windsor knot Tie knot credited to the British King, Edward VIII, later Duke of Windsor following his abdication, and made famous in the 1930s. It is a wide, triangular knot for a widespread shirt collar. The Half-Windsor is a less bulky knot, a medium-size symmetrical triangle for a standard shirt collar; it is also useful for a thick or wide tie which would be difficult to tie in a full Windsor.

Bibliography

This is a selected bibliography only.

Bennet-England, Rodney, *Dress Optional: the revolution in menswear* (Peter Owen, 1967)

Birnbach, Lisa, ed., *The Official Preppy Handbook* (Workman Publications, 1980)

Byrde, Penelope, *The Male Image* (Batsford)

A Cavalry Officer, *The Whole Art of Dress* (Effingham Wilson, 1830)

Cohn, David, L., *The Good Old Days, A History of American Morals and Manners as seen through the Sears Roebuck Catalogs* (Arno Press reprint, 1976)

Coleridge, Nicholas, *The Fashion Conspiracy* (Heinemann, 1988)

Colle, Doriece, *Collars, Stocks, Cravats* (Rodale Press, New York)

Cunnington, C. Willett and Phillis, *Handbook of English Costume in the 18th Century; Handbook of English Costume in the 19th Century* (Faber and Faber, 1973)

Cunnington, P. and A. Mansfield, *Handbook of English Costume in the 20th Century, 1900-1950* (Faber and Faber, 1973)

de Marly, Diana, *Fashion For Men: An Illustrated History* (Batsford, 1985)

Dyer, Rod and Ron Spark, *Fit To Be Tied: Vintage Ties of the Forties and Early Fifties* (Abbeville Press, 1987)

Laver, James, *The Tie* (Lewins)

Le Blanc, H., *The Art of Tying The Cravat (London, 1828).* See also *L'Art De Mettre Sa Cravate,* Baron L'Empese (Paris, 1927)

Major, The, *Clothes and the Man: Hints on the Wearing and Caring of Clothes* (London, 1900)

Moers, Eileen, *The Dandy* (Secker and Warburg, 1960)

Molloy, John T., *Dress For Success* (Warner Books, 1976)

Morse Earle, Alice, *Two Centuries of Costume in America 1620-1820* (Dover Publications, reprint, 1970)

Mosconi, David, and Villarosa, Riccardo, *The Book of Ties* (Tie Rack, London, 1985)

Murphy, Veronica, *The Dyed Textiles of India: Tradition and Trade* (Mapin, 1990)

The Neckwear Association of America, *Tie Buyer's Handbook* (New York)

Walker, R., *The Saville Row Story* (Prion, 1988)

Index

Acknowledgments

My special thanks to Madeleine Ginsburg, Rupert Radcliffe-Genge and Celestine Dars, who made this book possible; to Robert Gieve of Gieves and Hawkes, David Symons of T.M. Lewin and Company and Guy Fielding of the Dorset Institute for their generous help and advice; to Ian Bailey, Sandra Coe and Charles K. Bear for their research work; to Pierre Cardin, Richard Maddocks of Woodstock Neckwear in London and George Camacho of Burma Bibas in New York for explaining the licensing of designer ties; to the Trustees of the Mass Observation Archive for giving permission to quote from their unpublished material; to Gerald Andersen of The Neckwear Association of America Inc., Anthony Edwards of the Guild of British Tie Manufacturers and Myron Ackerman for their invaluable insights into the tie industry; to the Castle Howard Museum of Costume and Macclesfield Museums Trust in the North of England for giving me access to their fund of knowledge; and to Veronica Murphy of the Victoria and Albert Museum in London for her great kindness in allowing me to study the manuscript of her meticulous work on Indian textiles; and to Nigel Gee, Sheila Cook, Hermès and Martin Lawrence for loaning ties and scarfs, and providing photographs.